PRAI
LOVE, BOM.
AN FBI AGENT'S JOURNEY

"In his autobiographical book, Ken underlines his motivation and inspiration for his writing which is to help others think through what is real and what is fake news and alternative facts. His journey of over 40 years will answer the question: How does one of the FBI's first bomb technicians become the leading expert in the FBI BSU concerning the sexual victimization of children?"

— Ann W. Burgess, Professor
Boston College

"It is impossible to claim to be an expert in crimes against children, or "profiling," without having studied the writings of Ken Lanning. Reading *Love, Bombs, and Molesters: An FBI Agent's Journey*, the latest mesmerizing work by Kenneth V. Lanning, will tell you why this is undoubtedly true."

— Roger L. Depue, PhD
Former Chief of the FBI BSU

"It is an honor to get a glimpse of a life as interesting as Kenneth Lanning's. Ken worked tirelessly and selflessly for decades as an FBI special agent and consultant to combat crime, most notably crimes against children. In this engaging story of his personal and professional life, readers learn of the challenges and triumphs of his career and the overarching lessons he learned along the way — lessons that will help anyone think more critically. *Love, Bombs, and Molesters* is a thought-provoking page-turner and a fitting record of a life full of very good deeds."

— Bette L. Bottoms, Professor
University of Illinois at Chicago

"In the thousands of cases I've worked since taking Ken's class twenty-seven years ago, I've used what he taught, all the principles in this book, in every one of them, whether a child sexual assault case, a robbery, a murder, or petty crime."

— Joseph C. Stiles
Investigator, West Virginia Office of the Attorney General

Love, Bombs, and Molesters: An FBI Agent's Journey

By

Kenneth V. Lanning

Published by Kenneth Lanning
First trade paperback edition 2018
Printed in the United States of America

The names and identifying details of some characters in this book have been changed.

Although the author and publisher have made every effort to ensure the accuracy and completeness of information contained in this book, we assume no responsibility for errors, inaccuracies, omissions, or any inconsistency herein. Any slights of people, places, or organizations are unintentional.

The opinions expressed in this book are those of the author and not of the FBI.

Library of Congress Control Number: 2018904592

ISBN 978-0-692-11206-9

Copyediting by Daleen Berry
Cover design by Mary O'Sullivan
Text composition by Mary O'Sullivan

DEDICATION

      To Kathy, my wife of fifty years: You were the motivation for my journey. Without your support and companionship, I could not have maintained my balance and objectivity for all these years. Your greatest joy in life has been being a wife, mother ("Melissa" and "Rick"), and grandmother ("Max" "Brian" "Kyle") and taking care of your family and home. You did it all extremely well and you deserve your own Special Achievement Award for career accomplishments. Because you are the most humble and kind person I have ever met, you made me a better person along the way. Thank you for being my partner on our journey.

      To Melissa ("Missy Jane") and Rick ("Butchy Boy"), my children. I am so proud of you both. You have brought so much laughter and happiness to my life.

ACKNOWLEDGMENTS

In addition to the unfailing support of my parents, my wife and children, my extended family, and the Federal Bureau of Investigation (FBI), this publication would not be possible without the encouragement and assistance of many colleagues. Over the past sixty years, you have helped me on my journey and inspired me to tell my story in a way that I hope will entertain, influence and motivate others.

My knowledge and insight during my journey has been greatly influenced through my association and interaction with many people, some still living and others now dead. This includes:

My childhood friends, especially Terry Ward, Kathy Collins, Joan Marks, Roger Clancy, Ed Barnstorff, and Johnny Gallo; all the clergy and lay teachers who guided my Catholic education and nurtured my faith; my parish and school swimming coaches; and all those I served with in the Navy and Explosive Ordnance Disposal.

My colleagues in the FBI, especially Bill Beane, Jack Kirsch, Fred Smith, Chuck Killion, Ed Kelso, Loren Lee, Paul Hasselbach, Jon Wendt, Pat Cunningham, Jim Magee, Dennis Muehlstedt, Vince Doherty, Roger Young, Frank Sass, Leo Brunnick, Al MacDonald, and John Kirk. My colleagues in the FBI Behavioral Science & Behavioral Analysis Units, especially Roger Depue, Tony Rider, John Henry Campbell, Steve Etter, Larry Ankrom, Bob Ressler, John Douglas, Dick Ault, Jim Reese, Tom Strentz, Jim Horn, Blaine McIlwaine, Gregg McCrary, Mark Safarik, Bob Schaefer, Mark Hilts, Jim Beasley, Jim McNamara, Bill Hagmaier, Mary Ellen O'Toole, Jim Wright, Jim Clemente, Jennifer Eakin, Wayne Lord, Eileen Roemer, and particularly my BSU partner of many years Roy Hazelwood.

My law-enforcement colleagues, especially Bill Walsh, Donna Pence, Brian Killacky, Toby Tyler, Beth Dickinson, Bill Dworin, Bob

Hoever, Bob Farley, and Rick Cage; all my FBI National Academy students. My prosecutor colleagues, especially Paul Stern, Jim Peters, and Steve DeBrota.

My colleagues at the National Center for Missing & Exploited Children, especially John Rabun, Ruben Rodriquez, Pete Banks, and Terri Delaney. My noncriminal-justice colleagues, especially David Finkelhor, Ann Burgess, Lucy Berliner, Gail Goodman, Jon Conte, Bette Bottoms, Jan Hindman, Marilyn Grundy, and particularly Park Dietz.

Special thanks for assistance with organizing, editing, and writing this book go to Cindy Lent, Bette Bottoms, Jim Botting, Candace Conte, Sharon Clasen, and especially Mary O'Sullivan and Daleen Berry.

TABLE OF CONTENTS

And So it Begins

I cannot remember the exact date. At the time, I didn't recognize the significance of the phone call. I vividly recall its content – as if it happened just yesterday.

But it wasn't yesterday. It was more than thirty-five years ago – sometime in early 1983. While in my basement office in the converted bomb shelter at the Federal Bureau of Investigation (FBI) Academy in Quantico, Virginia, the telephone rang. Answering it, I found a law enforcement officer I'll call "Mike" from New England. He wanted my advice and guidance concerning an unusual case he was investigating. Mike had heard I was the FBI's behavioral expert on cases involving the sexual victimization of children and said his case involved a woman's allegations of sexual victimization as a young child. After spending many hours interviewing her, Mike was prompted to call me by some unusual aspects of the woman's allegations.

And so it begins.

I didn't know it then, but my journey as an FBI criminal "profiler" into evaluating complex allegations of bizarre ritual abuse of children and its subsequent effect on my career and life had just begun.

Unlike its portrayal in *Silence of the Lambs* or on the television program *Criminal Minds*, most of my operational work as an FBI profiler assigned to the Bureau's Behavioral Science Unit (BSU) was conducted over the telephone. As a matter of fact, for my twenty-fifth anniversary in the FBI, my BSU coworkers gave me a gag gift – a telephone receiver with a printed label acknowledgment: "To commemorate 25 years of dedicated service (13½ of which were spent on the phone!!)."

During that long ago call, Mike explained that the woman had only recently remembered the details of her victimization. Until a therapist helped her recover them, her memories had been repressed. Mike summarized for me the newfound memories she disclosed to him. Starting at a very young age, her parents and other adults who were all part of an organized satanic cult had sexually victimized her. She described how she and many other children were assaulted and abused during rituals involving strange ceremonies, drinking blood, eating flesh, and killing people. She said this cult activity went on for many years – and even continues today.

I was stunned and greatly concerned by such horrific allegations. Other than their extreme nature, I had no reason to believe that the alleged crimes had not taken place. If true, that was clearly one of the worst cases of child sexual abuse I had ever heard of during my then ten years of studying sex crimes. I was so concerned that I was determined to do everything I possibly could to help stop, catch, and convict the offenders.

Mike asked if I had ever heard of cases involving such severe elements of sexual abuse and if I could recommend any specific investigative responses. I told him I knew of cases involving **each** element of the allegations, but had never heard of one involving **all** of them together. I clearly remember telling him that even after all these years, evidence of much of the activity should still exist. We talked about getting as many specific details as possible from the victim, and then trying to corroborate the various elements.

We both recognized the value of identifying the adult accomplices and trying to get them to turn against one another. This is a common investigative technique in multiple-offender, conspiracy-type cases. Other than using those basic investigative techniques and suggesting he get additional manpower and resources, I didn't have any special insights or brilliant recommendations.

I wish I could have provided more help as I asked Mike to keep me posted about his progress. As I hung up the phone, I remember thinking that the case was shocking and terrible, but fortunately very rare. I assumed that in my entire career as an FBI profiler, I would probably never hear of another one quite like it.

I soon discovered how wrong I was.

Within a matter of weeks, I received a phone call from "Bette," a professional colleague and attorney. She also knew of my specialized work in the FBI concerning crimes against children. Bette was calling for a female friend, who wanted an expert's advice before deciding whether to go to the police with some shocking information about her own childhood sexual victimization. Bette's friend told her about extreme abuse that went way beyond any case of child sexual abuse that Bette knew about. Her friend described being sexually victimized by multiple offenders who were part of a highly organized satanic cult, abuse which included rituals involving strange ceremonies, drinking blood, eating flesh, and killing people.

I immediately recalled my conversation with Mike. As Bette talked, I searched for my notes from that consultation. When I found them, I told Bette that I was already aware of this case and had talked to the investigating officer. But Bette said that was impossible – because her friend had never spoken to anyone in law enforcement. As I compared the two cases, I realized there were some other differences, including their locations. This one occurred in the Mid-Atlantic area, the first one in New England. And in the second case, the victim had always been aware of the abuse, so it wasn't a repressed memory later recovered during therapy.

That's when it dawned on me: Could there possibly be two such similar, horrific cases? If so, were they somehow connected?

Almost immediately, I began a quest to understand these difficult cases. I quickly realized that if I was going to professionally evaluate cases like these, I needed to know far more about Satanism than what I'd learned in religion and theology classes during my sixteen years of education in Catholic schools.

I first learned about the spirit creature known as the Devil from the nuns who taught me in Catholic grammar school. I learned that the Devil, or Satan, was also called Lucifer - the fallen angel. Lucifer had once been one of God's favorite angels, but then he challenged God's authority. As quoted from Milton's *Paradise Lost*, "better to reign in Hell, than serve in Heaven." In the ensuing battle, St. Michael the Archangel defeated Lucifer and cast him into Hell. From there, I learned, the devil continues to tempt humans to commit sin and join him in Hell.

What of St. Michael the Archangel? For Catholics, he is the patron saint of law enforcement. As time went on, I would hear more nuanced versions of this theology in Catholic high school and college. All of my religious education, however, was of little value in conducting an investigation into criminal activity. Unfortunately for me, it provided no objective investigative insight into the two cases I was then challenged with understanding and helping to solve.

So like Lewis and Clark, I embarked on a journey of discovery that would forever change not only my professional but also my personal life. I would never again view and evaluate information the same way. Even today, hardly a day goes by that I don't think about the importance of what I learned during the years that followed those phone calls. That journey taught me a great deal about investigating and evaluating allegations of criminal behavior. It also helped me appreciate, almost to a fault, the importance of definitions and how to keep an open mind about life's important issues – and thus make better decisions.

That's why I wrote this book. I wasn't interested in writing a mere collection of war stories for laypeople, about cases I had worked during my twenty years in the FBI BSU, or those I've consulted on since retiring in 2000. I've already done that, in a way, since during my career I wrote many publications for professionals about the sexual victimization of children (*see* Appendix III). The National Center for Missing & Exploited Children (NCMEC) has disseminated over 250,000 printed copies of one such widely used publication, *Child Molesters: A Behavioral Analysis*. Another, titled *Investigator's Guide to Allegations of "Ritual" Child Abuse*, is frequently cited and has been widely circulated on the Internet.

Books about FBI profiling work tended to use words like *Darkness, Evil, Monster, Hunter,* and *Predator* in the title. I didn't want my book title to focus on such emotion-laden, one-dimensional terms. I wasn't even sure I wanted to write a book. If I did decide to write one, though, it would be largely to satisfy the many people who have asked about the story of my career.

I wanted a compelling title, one that would create interest in my journey – a lifelong trek that began when I fell in love and wanted to get married, then became a Navy Explosive Ordnance Disposal (EOD) technician, next one of the first FBI bomb technicians, and finally the leading expert concerning the sexual victimization of children in the BSU. Thus the title: *Love, Bombs, and Molesters: An FBI Agent's Journey*.

But just telling my story wasn't enough. I also wanted the book to be relevant and find a wider audience beyond readers simply interested in true-crime stories. In this autobiography, I describe how certain events in my early life led me first to the Navy, then to the FBI. I tell how those events influenced my perspectives. More important, I discuss how my FBI experience with what came to be called "satanic ritual abuse" changed the way I looked at every one of my cases, and eventually all the information I synthesized, whether in private or public, personally or professionally.

Although I describe my professional experience with child sexual victimization allegations, those cases aren't my real focus. I discuss them to share my insight with you, but mostly to explain the mental evaluation process I used in reaching my conclusions. My hope is that my experiences will help you to better identify fake news and alternative facts, think about how you process and circulate information, and improve how you form opinions and make decisions (whether liberal or conservative in orientation) about important issues such as healthcare reform, climate change, voting, gun violence, and personal finances.

In summary, the key insights I gained throughout my decades of experience, and want to share, are as follows:

(1) Life events are interconnected, and there are many forks in the road on the journey.

(2) Adults tend to believe what they want or need to believe, and the greater the need, the greater the tendency.

(3) Referring to the same thing by different names or different things by the same name, frequently creates confusion.

(4) Although the exact procedure will vary, the same basic process that I used in my professional investigations can apply to making major life decisions.

Whenever possible, I avoid naming names or citing the details of specific, identifiable cases. The behaviors I describe are not unique to any one individual, group, or case and my conclusions are not based on a few isolated incidents or cases. They are based on the sum total of my forty plus years of professional experience in evaluating information. As I tell my story about how our background and needs influence our objectivity, I fully recognize that I am equally vulnerable to and influenced by all the biases I seek to understand, illuminate, and share with you.

So, "caveat emptor" – or, buyer beware!

CHAPTER ONE

"Because I Wanted to Get Married"

During my more than forty years spent studying the criminal aspects of child sexual victimization, the running and dark joke within my family is that *perversion* is my life. Like other people in professional fields similar to child sexual abuse, I have repeatedly heard: "How did you wind up specializing in this area?" and "How have you lasted so long?"

I'm not sure I know the complex answers to these questions, but I've come to believe that the historical narrative of how my life unfolded is revealing. Life's journey is often not a straight path, but a series of forks in the road. Each bend you take leads you to something that is often not anticipated or recognized as significant at the time. That's what happened to me. So when someone asks how I got involved in this work, I often enticingly answer, *"Because I wanted to get married."*

I was born and raised in the Bronx in New York City. Since I was born in 1944, I am technically not a baby boomer, with all the associated stereotypes. During the 1950s, my Bronx neighborhood was almost like Mayberry, from *The Andy Griffith Show*. It essentially was a middle-class, mostly Irish-Catholic, ethnic neighborhood in the middle of New York City. At the time, there were no violent gangs or serious crime. While there was plenty of alcohol available, it was easy to avoid taking illegal drugs because none of my friends nor I had the slightest idea where to find them. The only guns I ever saw while growing up were in the holsters of the police officers who stood guard at the polling place each Election Day. Everyone in my neighborhood pretty much knew everyone else. When I was in the eighth grade, I once smoked a few cigarettes on a secluded side street not far from our apartment. Before I arrived home that day, a neighbor had already informed my mother.

Our neighborhood was like a small town defined by the boundaries of our Roman Catholic parish church, St. Nicholas of Tolentine – usually identified simply as "Tolentine." The parish center was a complex of buildings consisting of two schools, two convents, a rectory, and a large commanding church known as "The Cathedral of the Bronx" with another church, almost as large, beneath it. Numerous masses and other religious services were held in both churches, and thousands of parishioners went to Mass every Sunday. Many of them also went during the week – especially during Lent.

Although the 1950s are sometimes inaccurately idealized, my family was in fact very much like *Father Knows Best* – except without the single-family house. We lived in a three-bedroom rent-controlled apartment on the second floor of a five-story apartment building. I could easily relate to much about how life was portrayed on the 1950s sitcoms, but we didn't have a house or a backyard. Because of that, I identified more with *I Love Lucy* until the Ricardos moved to their new house in Connecticut. But in essence, I lived the 1950s childhood that some people now claim never existed.

I was born into a stable, traditional family. My father was from a working-class Irish-Catholic family. My mother came from a working-class Scot-German-Protestant family. For the most part, I was the descendant of recent immigrants. My maternal grandmother was born in Scotland; my maternal grandfather's parents were from Germany; and my paternal grandmother's parents were born in Ireland. The Lanning branch of my family has been here in the United States (U.S.) since the Revolutionary War. I was a middle child with three sisters – two older, Barbara and Joan, and one younger, Terry. We were raised with no firm ethnic identities other than that of being plain American. My father worked hard to support our family and my mother was a stay-at-home mom. This was true of the vast majority of the families in my neighborhood.

Although I didn't meet her until I was in college, my future wife, Kathy, grew up in a similar family in a neighborhood on the west side of the same parish. With loving parents, she was the middle of seven children born over twenty years. Being teased by her three older siblings and helping to care for her three younger siblings made Kathy the great wife and mother she would later become. Our dates frequently included babysitting her four-year-old sister. We would also occasionally drive her mother in my VW bug to the Manhattan bank, where she sometimes worked the midnight shift. I would later be welcomed into her family and she into mine. I grew up with no brothers. However, between the husbands of my three sisters, those of Kathy's three sisters, as well as her three brothers, I wound up with nine brothers-in-law.

My father sometimes worked three jobs, especially around Christmas time, so my mother did not have to work any jobs (outside the home). We lived happily within our means and my father never borrowed money. He didn't even have a checking account. Early on, I learned that a real man is one who takes care of his family. On the weekends, when we were young children, my father regularly took us to the Bronx Zoo. To qualify as informed New Yorkers, on our Circle Line Boat trips around Manhattan Island, he taught us the names of all the bridges we passed under. A favorite trip for me was the Third Ave El all the way from Fordham Road in the Bronx to South Ferry at the southern tip of Manhattan. I would stand at the front window in the first car pretending I was driving the train. After arriving at South Ferry, we took a round-trip ferry ride to Staten Island across New York harbor and past the Statue of Liberty. The cost for the full days' train and ferry ride for our entire family was just a few dollars. Other cherished memories with my father involve baseball games at the Polo Grounds and Yankee Stadium, where I still hear the voice of public address announcer Bob Sheppard and once believed Babe Ruth and Lou Gehrig were buried under the center field monuments. At the end of a game, my father and I would walk from home plate to center field in "the house that Ruth built."

Something like domestic violence was unthinkable in my home. My father emphatically taught me that a boy/man never ever hits a girl/woman. As a young boy with three sisters, that lesson was sometimes a challenge. My younger sister, Terry, who was almost as big as me when we were young, would frequently take advantage of the protection this afforded her. Even though it sometimes meant enduring a few smacks, I never disobeyed my father's instructions to not ever hit a girl. My parents modeled and instilled in me a sense of honor and duty. They were happy, mature adults who taught us values, the concept of right and wrong, and a sense of responsibility. More important, they not only taught it – they lived it.

One year for Christmas my sisters and I got a bicycle. Because I was the only boy outnumbered three to one, Santa Claus brought us a girl's bicycle. My sisters and I shared it for the next several years. As another Christmas approached, my father actually came to me apologizing about something he had to do. He explained that I was getting older and he wanted me to have a boy's bicycle. But he couldn't afford a new one so he bought a used one. He spent hours in the basement of our apartment building, secretly fixing and cleaning it for me. I was going to get it for Christmas and he wanted me to know why it was not new. It was all he could afford, but the work he put into it and the talk we had that day made it priceless. Like Ralphie's Red Ryder BB Gun in *A Christmas Story*, it was the greatest Christmas present I ever received – and the only one I vividly remember to this day. It influenced me deeply; causing me to believe that children turn out best when their parents give them everything they can afford as long as everything they can give is not too much.

Not having a backyard, my childhood friends and I spent endless hours playing a wide variety of street games. There were no video games, Internet, or social media. Street games such as ring-a-levio, three-steps-to-Germany, spud, chicken-in-the coop, baby-bases, Johnny-ride-a-pony, hide-and-go-seek, salugee, tag, box ball, running bases, hit the stick, two-hand touch football, and many others consumed our free time. Today some of these games would be considered politically incorrect or even as forms of bullying. For instance, "sounding" which was a verbal duel of insults with your friends, was an acquired skill and a way to achieve status among your peers. A regular street mantra back then was "Sticks and stones may break my bones, but names will never hurt me." Our favorite game was *stickball*, a version of baseball. With a broom handle taken from your apartment building basement, a "Spaldeen" high bounce pink rubber ball, and a skill for dodging passing cars; we played stickball in the street for hours.

There was no adult supervision or umpires, which reduced the pressure and taught us the need to follow self-enforced rules. You could strike out with the bases loaded and suffer little humiliation. You had to accept the fielder calling an "out" or the game was over. Catching a ball that bounced off a parked car was by our rules a double. The feat of hitting the ball onto the roof of a neighborhood six-story apartment building was ruled a home run. If, however, the kid who owned the ball called "chips," whoever hit it on a roof or lost it down a sewer had to pay him twenty-five cents for a new one. Believe it or not, back in the1950s, police officers would frequently try to stop us from playing stickball by confiscating our bats. We quickly learned that showing the police respect and cooperating with whatever they asked was the best way to avoid bigger problems. Growing up then on the streets of the Bronx was not especially dangerous, but it did teach you to be self-sufficient and resourceful, and toughened you for real world challenges.

Religion was an important moral compass in my childhood. My father's Catholic faith was something he lived by, but not something by which he judged others. I have met few people during my lifetime with the character, sense of humor, dedication, and devotion he had. My father always put his family first; with his only indulgence I can recall being an FM radio he bought himself so he could relax to the easy-listening format then broadcast on WPAT-FM from New Jersey. He finally saved enough money and bought the radio shortly before he died in 1962. All my life I have tried to do the right thing as if my father was watching. During my mini mid-life crisis, at age fifty, I bought myself a red Miata sports car. But I soon sold it because I would regularly hear my father's voice saying, "only a selfish man would buy a small car that he couldn't use to help out others by giving them rides." My pangs of guilt continued – until I finally sold my Miata.

I realize that my father's strong feelings about the size of cars might have been influenced in part by the fact that, as many living in New York City, we never owned a car. We usually had to rely on friends and relatives to take us on our annual family vacations to Freehold in the Catskill Mountains, in upstate New York. Freehold was just two miles from East Durham in the heart of the Irish Catskills. Going to Sunday Mass at Our Lady of Knock Church in East Durham was different from Mass at Tolentine in the Bronx. The church was so small it filled up quickly, with the many Irish vacationers. Therefore, our attendance often consisted of standing in the grass outside. We stayed at a boarding house formally named *The Freehold House*, but known to all as Parks' after the owner Jenny Parks. There was no air conditioning, only a pitcher and basin in each room, a shared bathroom down the hall, and swimming was in the local creek where we also bathed. But those who spent their summers there in the 1950s will never forget it. There was a memorable tradition of ringing the bell that called us to meals, as each family left for home at the end of their vacation.

On one such summer vacation, when I was about seven years old and had not yet learned to swim, I was floating on an inner tube in Barlow's Creek in East Durham. A teenage boy was horsing around when he suddenly flipped my inner tube over. I can vividly remember sinking down, down, down. As I looked up through the flowing water, I saw my mother's image fading away. I was frightened and thought I was drowning. I clearly remember being under the water for several minutes – until my mother's arm reached down and grabbed me. The scary memory of this event is still clear in my mind more than sixty-five years later.

The only problem is, most it never happened. I know this because I have been back to this spot many times – and analyzed what could have actually happened. My tube did flip over, but I could not have been going "down, down, down" – because the water at that spot is less than three feet deep. I could not have been under the water for more than a few seconds before my mother pulled me up. I later learned that this is an anecdotal example of something called a "false" or "pseudo" memory. It wasn't a lie when I told other people about it, but it certainly wasn't accurate.

As a child, my family's social life revolved around our parish Catholic Church and its parochial schools. My sisters and I all attended those parish-run parochial schools (grammar and high school) for one dollar a month, a fee charged only for the oldest child in each family. That's because each Sunday's donations paid for the schools. Each day we walked the short distance from home to school. The Dominican nuns of Blauvelt taught both girls and boys mixed together in grammar school, which went from first to eighth grade. When we got to high school, the girls and boys were separated into classrooms on different floors. The Dominican nuns taught the girls and the Augustinian priests taught the boys – supplemented by lay teachers. I looked forward to the Friday night dances each week, which were held in the school auditorium for the high school students. Adult chaperones made sure there was room for the Holy Ghost between the couples dancing during the 10:00 p.m. "slowathon," when they played ten slow songs in a row.

My life in Catholic school was probably made easier by three factors. First, I was essentially an obedient and compliant child. Second, I was a good student, most often having the highest grades in my class. Third, at the time, I honestly believed, and told my second grade teacher that I wanted to be a priest. That information apparently made its way to each of my subsequent teachers. During the 1950s, among Catholics and my teachers, most of whom were nuns, becoming a priest was a revered vocation to be nurtured and encouraged.

I received a great education in spite of the fact that there were probably at least forty-five students in all my grammar school classes and there was no preschool or kindergarten. Of course, the ability to learn in that kind of school environment required the presence of effective discipline and involved parents who valued education.

The corner candy stores ("Lujacks"), and later, the neighborhood bars ("Mannions"), were important aspects of the social structure, but in a sense they too were integrated into activities focused around the church. I took for granted the bakeries ("Webers") we visited after Mass each Sunday, the delicatessens ("Bobs") we went to for meatball heroes at lunchtime during high school, and the pizza places ("Jimmys") we went to after the Friday night dance for a slice and a Coke costing a quarter. I didn't truly appreciate them until I moved out of the Bronx in 1967. For the next few years, whenever I returned to the Bronx to visit my mother and sisters, I usually stopped into Weber's Bakery and bought a big birthday cake decorated with roses, even though it wasn't anyone's birthday. Years later, when I returned in 1984 to testify about child molesters before the Bronx County Special Grand jury, my Bronx roots were still on my mind. The FBI agent who picked me up at the airport said I was early and asked if there was anything I wanted to do before testifying. I said I wanted to go to Jimmy's Pizza Place on Fordham Road and get a slice and a coke. It was the first **real** pizza I had in years.

Major life events, such as First Communion, Confirmation, school, graduation, Friday night dances, dating, and holiday celebrations, were all connected to the parish church in one way or another. The Church had social as well as religious significance. Until I was twenty-one years old, I had never been more than 125 miles from my Bronx neighborhood. Growing up, almost everyone I knew and interacted with was Catholic. Interestingly, one exception was my mother and my maternal grandparents.

Although my mother did everything she could to ensure my sisters and I complied with Catholic teaching and schooling, she herself was a Presbyterian. When I was a teenager, my mother would occasionally explain to me some of the differences between the religious practices in Catholic and Protestant churches – including more congregational singing by Protestants. In theory, today there is more singing at Catholic mass but most of it seems to consist of mumbling by the congregation led by the voice of one parish member who is an unfulfilled music major. I also remember my maternal grandfather (my "Pop Pop") once voicing his disappointment since each of his three faithful Protestant children had married Catholics and had to agree to raise his grandchildren as Catholics. He couldn't understand what difference it made. Although my mother was involved in many parish activities and most Tolentine parishioners believed she was a Catholic, she never converted. After my father died and my sisters and I grew up as Catholic, my mother once again actively practiced her Protestant faith.

My Catholic school education continued to play a role in my later life. After I retired from the FBI, I was retained as an expert in numerous civil lawsuits involving sexual victimization of children resulting from possible negligence by organizations that served youths. This included the Catholic Church. An attorney who wanted to hire me asked me if my Roman Catholic upbringing made me biased for or against the Church. It was a thought-provoking question. To what extent does our personal background affect our opinions and conclusions? My experience in Catholic schools was very positive and I extensively discuss the issue of bias in later chapters. I do know that the Catholic education I received served me well in my adult life, both in graduate school and in my jobs with the U.S. Navy, FBI, and as a private consultant.

Much of the education I received was viewed through the prism of the Catholic Church. In my youth, it was a conservative, staunchly anti-communist institution. In 1956, there was a revolt against the Communist government in Hungary, then controlled by the Soviet Union. During this brief revolution, Catholic Cardinal Jozsef Mindszenty, who had been tortured and sentenced to life imprisonment by the "godless communists," was freed. When the Soviets invaded and crushed the revolution, Cardinal Mindszenty took refuge in the U.S. Embassy. He lived there for the next fifteen years. At the time, I was in seventh grade. We all took a vow to say prayers every day, until Hungary was free of evil communist oppression. That took another thirty-five years to happen, and I had often forgotten to say those prayers. I sometimes wondered if my spiritual lapse played any role in the long delay.

One of my Spanish teachers was a priest whom the former dictator Fidel Castro had expelled from Communist Cuba. If we had not done our homework, we could always delay the day's lesson by asking him, "Was it true that Castro was really doing good things in Cuba?" For the remainder of the class, he passionately discussed the evils of Castro and Communism. He sometimes showed us films of hearings before the House Committee on Un-American Activities, and spoke of their value in identifying godless communists in the U.S.

This educational perspective also influenced my views about historical events such as the Inquisition, the defeat of the Spanish Armada, and the Protestant Reformation. When I watched the Errol Flynn swashbuckling movies as a boy, I found myself rooting for the Catholic Spanish to defeat the Protestant English. Some of what I was taught is inconsistent with what is commonly accepted today. For instance, when I learned about the Spanish Civil War of the 1930s, Generalissimo Franco was presented as one of the historical good guys, because he had defended the Catholic Church against the extreme leftist government. Although Franco was supported by Nazi Germany, I was taught that he led a righteous rebellion against a worse Marxist government supported by the Communist Soviet Union.

In addition, the efforts of Senator Joseph McCarthy and the House Committee on Un-American Activities to identify communists in the 1950s were presented to us as good, patriotic, and pro-Catholic actions. Protestants were not viewed as bad people – good news since my mother was one. They were Christians who just went too far in addressing some excesses in the one, true Roman Catholic Church.

I didn't blindly accept everything I was taught in school. For example, I remember being repeatedly taught in history classes that the Boston Massacre in 1770 involved British soldiers who shot unarmed, innocent American patriots without justification. But I also remember watching an episode of the Walter Cronkite-hosted television program *You are There* that reenacted the Boston Massacre. This program set forth in great visual and verbal detail the events that took place that day. As I watched the program, I clearly remember thinking to myself that the so-called patriots who were shot that day were not innocent bystanders. They may not have had firearms, but they provoked and aggressively threatened the lives of the soldiers and disobeyed lawful orders. I felt that what the British soldiers did was self-defense and clearly justified. As a young schoolboy, I assumed that this television program must be accurate. Yet, I couldn't understand why my teachers had not presented the event the same way. I was afraid to confront them with my confusion, or ask about these variations.

Years later I learned that, at their trial, John Adams (who later became the second U.S. President) successfully defended the British soldiers who had committed that so-called massacre. They were acquitted. This later information I acquired was not consistent with what I learned in school. But it was consistent with a TV program. This amended and well-documented knowledge, along with factual research, helped change my opinions. I was learning that important decisions need to be based on objective study, but when confronted with new facts it was perfectly acceptable to change your mind. I was already searching for the facts. As Sgt. Joe Friday supposedly said on the 1950s *Dragnet* TV show I regularly watched, "Just the facts, Ma'am."

On my campus at Manhattan College in the early 1960s, some protestors against growing U.S. involvement in the Vietnam War entered the Administration Building – not to take it over, but to seek protection from the vast majority of students trying to run them off the campus. By the mid 1960s, my Church seemed to transform radically before my eyes, almost overnight. This was due to ceremonial religious changes mandated by the Second Vatican Council (1962-1965) and sweeping cultural changes.

Around that same time, during the afternoon of November 22, 1963, as I was walking on the Manhattan College campus, a fellow student told me that President Kennedy, the first Catholic President, had been assassinated. I still clearly remember the shock I felt at hearing that shattering news, which shook me to the core of my Irish-Catholic roots.

By the time the 1970s arrived, I was in the FBI – and even Catholic priests and nuns were protesting the Vietnam War.

At the same time they protested military action taken against the communists, they were supporting a radical leftist political philosophy in other parts of the world. Some called this liberation theology. Others called it Christianized Marxism. I had no problem with peaceful and legal protest, but these Catholic clerics were breaking into government offices and damaging government property, and as an FBI agent I was assigned to investigate them and their crimes. This challenged my father's rules for my childhood about obeying such religious clerics and my religious beliefs about their divine vocations.

In the mid 1970s, I visited my mother at my former Catholic high school in the Bronx. By then, she was working as a secretary there and soon introduced me to a new, young priest on the faculty. She told him I was an FBI agent. I assumed because of FBI efforts to investigate and arrest some anti-war Catholic clerics, he responded that he guessed he could still shake my hand and talk to me in spite of that. By then I was dealing with priests who were anti-government radicals and child molesters, so I looked him in the eye and said I guessed I could still shake his hand and talk to him, even though he was a Catholic priest. It was difficult for me to believe the Church I knew and that nurtured me could have changed so dramatically in such a short time.

The more I learned about the details of the Church's sexual abuse scandal, the worse my disappointment got. I knew nothing about child sexual abuse or sex crimes as a child. No one in my family had ever been a victim of sexual abuse. I certainly had never been molested. And I knew of no one else who had been, either. I do vaguely recall my mother telling me, when, as a young boy I went out to play, to "watch out for the gypsies." I had no idea what she was talking about. From television shows I then watched, gypsies seemed to be a group people who wore unusual hats and rode around in horse-drawn wagons with a covering like the pitched roof of a house. I had never seen anyone who looked like that. My mother never explained, and I never asked why I should watch out for them.

But, I later learned that her warning was a leftover remnant of the common practice of accusing unusual and feared sub-cultures of engaging in extreme behavior, such as blood rituals and stealing children. Hence the term *witch hunt*. I believe her warning was probably a holdover from my mother's own childhood.

Based on what I later came to learn in my FBI work, however, I now suspect that there may have been a few adults in my childhood neighborhood whose interest in children was probably "too good to be true." Some of those "nice guys" might even have had a sexual interest in children. Back then in my world, such things were not typically recognized or even mentioned. We certainly knew of no scandals involving priests sexually abusing children. The closest anyone came to discussing that was when the nuns occasionally told adolescent girls in the high school, "don't hang all over Father; he's only a man." How this might affect Father was not clearly stated, but certainly implied. There was, in fact, one parish priest who appeared to be romantically interested in an attractive girl who was a senior in the High School. I later learned he left the priesthood and married her. Back then; no one considered the possibility that young children or adolescent boys might sexually arouse "Father."

For personal and selfish reasons, I am happy and grateful that child sexual abuse allegations at the hands of priests were not part of my childhood. My father was a traditional, devout Roman Catholic who sincerely believed that priests were engaged in a God-given vocation. His view of priests, and to a lesser extent my own view, was embodied in his two favorite movies; both were required viewing growing up in our home – *Boys Town* with Spencer Tracy and *Going My Way* with Bing Crosby. Tracy played Father Flanagan, and Crosby played Father O'Malley – good, decent, and inspirational priests. My father's favorite charities were Father Flanagan's Boys Town with the statue out front bearing the inscription, "He ain't heavy Father, he's m' brother" and the Maryknoll Fathers and Brothers. I know my father would have been devastated, had he ever learned of such sex scandals.

And while I sincerely know how much my father loved me, if I ever had to tell him a priest had molested me, he would have been placed in the unbearable situation of having to choose between believing his son – or following his faith. Fortunately, this dilemma never occurred in our family. But it did occur in many others. I went on to Catholic college, where I developed a more complex faith – and understanding that the offenses and actions of some priests do not negate the good work of most priests or an entire religion. To varying degrees, all the priests, brothers, and nuns from my childhood were a positive influence in my life. Some of those I encountered in my adult professional life were another matter.

One Tolentine parish priest in particular had more of a positive, far-reaching influence on my life than anyone except my parents. This Augustinian priest, whom I'll call Father "Quinn," came to the parish when I was in the fifth grade, and soon organized a swimming team for the parish children. I tried out and made the team.

Today, people only a few years younger than me are surprised and shocked when I reveal that when I began competitive swimming in the mid-1950s, boys (unlike girls) were not allowed to wear bathing suits in certain indoor pools designated for boys. It was known as swimming "BA" or "Bare Ass." My Catholic school did not have a swimming pool, so we practiced at a nearby public high school. This New York City public school had such a rule. Fr. Quinn, the priest who was our coach, had no control over it. To the best of my recollection, we were told that this rule was because the lint from our bathing suits would clog the swimming pool filter. (Of course, no one ever explained why this didn't happen with girls' bathing suits in their pool.)

Although boys regularly showered together naked, standing around the pool deck for long periods of time without a bathing suit was both awkward and uncomfortable. As typical adolescent boys, keeping your eyes up and focused forward became an important aspect of pool etiquette, as it was with urinal etiquette. Thankfully, this issue was resolved in the late 1950s when the Speedo-type bathing suit was developed for competitive swimmers. Although I was never an elite swimmer, I swam competitively in grammar school and high school, and was the captain and outstanding swimmer on my

Manhattan College swim team. Back then you only got a medal or trophy for finishing first, second, or third, and I won a bunch of them as a breast-stroke specialist. I loved swimming so much, and spent so much time in the water, that when I later entered the U.S. Navy, I wanted to become a diver.

Father Quinn was also the best and most influential teacher I ever had. He played a major role in putting me on the path toward academic excellence. He even arranged for me to obtain a combination swimming and academic scholarship to Villanova University in Pennsylvania. After my father died, Father Quinn helped my mother get her secretarial job at the parish high school. In the late 1980s, I learned that this Augustinian priest was living in retirement in his religious order's monastery at Villanova University. I traveled to the University because I wanted to personally thank him for what he meant to me and the role he played in how well my life turned out. He was now old and almost blind but he vividly remembered my family and me. We reminisced about his time at Tolentine parish and with unbelievable accuracy he could still remember coaching decisions he had made at swim meets thirty years earlier.

In 2014, I was devastated to learn that Fr. Quinn, who had been a coach, teacher, mentor, and family friend was credibly accused of sexually victimizing numerous young girls in my old parish in the Bronx and in another parish in the Boston area. Because he and the allegations were very old when they became known, he was never criminally prosecuted. He died a short time later. This only reinforced what I had by then come to know from my work in the FBI and will discuss later in this book about *nice guy* child molesters. This priest was not pretending to be nice to gain access to children; he was nice. But he also apparently was a child molester.

The bubble of my almost idealic childhood burst when my father died from cancer in 1962. I was seventeen and a high school senior. My family was never the same after that. There were no more traditional family dinners or cherished summer vacations to Freehold in the Catskill Mountains. One of the greatest regrets of my life is that I never got to know and talk to him as an adult. Because my widowed mother was then alone, I changed my plans about going away to college at Villanova University in Philadelphia. Instead, I enrolled in Manhattan College, a Catholic college located in the Bronx, and commuted to class each day from the apartment where I had grown up. During my senior year in college, I began dating Kathy, the woman I would eventually marry. She was from my Bronx parish and a few years younger than me. Our romance began on a Labor Day weekend in Rockaway, New York in 1965. Rockaway, in the City borough of Queens, was on the beach and was filled with Irish bars and summer cottages. It was the other major vacation spot for the New York City Irish.

At the time, the war in Vietnam was also raging, but since I was a college student, I had a draft deferment. Back then you had to register for the draft when you turned eighteen. Everyone I knew eagerly complied because the draft card you received was the proof you needed to legally drink in a New York bar. I realized, however, that after I graduated in June 1966, I would have to do something about my military obligation or be drafted.

For me, something like running off to Canada or burning my draft card was never an option. I was also not interested in going to graduate school just to continue my student deferment. Rather than waiting to be drafted, I decided to voluntarily join the military. I also thought it would be better to serve as an officer than as an enlisted man and less risky to serve in the Navy or Air Force rather than the Army or Marines. I didn't believe that wanting to increase my chances of survival made me a coward or un-American – and had I been sent into combat, I would have gone willingly.

But when I went to join, I discovered that the Air Force was only interested in new officers who could be pilots. The Navy also would immediately take my application and process me – but only if I qualified to fly. For anyone wanting to become a regular line officer, they took your name and put it on a long waiting list keeping you in limbo until a future testing date. That's what they did with me. Although I never wanted to be a pilot, as a back up I still applied to take the Navy pilot test. I scored very high on the general intelligence part of the test, but not on the second pilot aptitude part. For the first time in my life I had failed a test. My military career as a pilot was over before it began. I was never going to be a *Top Gun* Navy pilot.

Just before I was about to apply to the Army or Marines, the Navy finally notified me of a test date to qualify to attend Navy Officer Candidate School (OCS) for line officers. I eventually took the tests with over a hundred other college seniors from the New York metropolitan area. At the time, the Navy could be so selective that only two people in my entire group received passing scores. Fortunately, I was one of them. I completed a mountain of paperwork and was ultimately told to report to OCS in Newport, Rhode Island, in October 1966 after I graduated from college in June. My girlfriend, Kathy, and I soon began talking about getting married after I completed OCS. We decided, however, to delay any final decision until after I received my commission as a Navy Ensign and got my first duty station assignment.

Before reporting to OCS, I had naively assumed that being a Naval officer meant reporting each morning to my ship and then going home each evening to my family. I guess I thought it was like a yacht club. In hindsight, it is still hard for me to believe how I could have been so naive. Maybe it was what I wanted to believe. When I got to OCS, we were quickly told that a shore duty assignment was highly unlikely for a newly commissioned officer. We were advised that anyone planning to get married would be wise to delay such plans. You would not be seeing your new wife very much because your first assignment would most likely be aboard a ship that would be deployed for eighteen months to two years away from the United States. I was stunned, and was slowly growing depressed about our plans to get married.

Then, during the second week of the sixteen-week OCS program, we were marched over to listen to a series of presentations about optional volunteer programs available to newly commissioned Navy Reserve officers. One, an Explosive Ordnance Disposal (EOD) program, involved almost one full year of training to be a diver and to dismantle military munitions (bombs, mines and torpedoes) and improvised explosive devices. Although I was not sure I wanted to "render safe" (as it is referred to in this line of work) explosive devices, the training period would at least guarantee some shore duty and time with a new wife. I was also drawn to it because all the officers accepted into this program would be trained in Key West, Florida to be Navy divers. I had been a competitive swimmer since grammar school and for a long time imagined becoming a Navy frogman. There was also a presentation that day on the Navy SEALs program, but I knew from my prior inquiries about frogmen that their selection process and basic training would be more physically demanding than I could probably handle. At the time I was 5' 10" tall and weighed about 130 lbs.

Both Navy EOD and Navy SEALs ("frogmen") involve explosives and being a Navy diver. EOD is primarily a defensive military asset (rendering safe explosive devices), whereas SEALs are primarily an offensive military asset (planting explosive devices, eliminating terrorists). Both are psychologically and intellectually demanding. They are both important military resources, with the Navy SEALs being more physically focused and Navy EOD being more academically focused. Most of the EOD training was in the classroom. Some personnel are qualified in both. People today are certainly more aware of the Navy SEALs as a result of the movie *American Sniper* and their skill and courage in the killing of Osama bin Laden and their other anti-terrorism missions.

As I said, back at this time I knew about frogmen, but I had never heard of "Explosive Ordnance Disposal." Most Americans knew little about this military program until the movie *The Hurt Locker*, about Army EOD in Iraq, won the 2009 Academy Award for Best Picture. At the end of this OCS presentation about EOD back in 1966, I rushed up to get more information. I asked what would happen if at the end of the one-year training you changed your mind about being in the program. They said it was a totally voluntary program and you could opt out at anytime. If you did so, the Bureau of Navy Personnel would then give you a new assignment. For me the decision was made: if accepted into this EOD program, I knew I would have about one year to be with my new wife. That was then my foremost concern.

I immediately volunteered for the program, but obviously was not yet accepted. Later that afternoon, I had to report along with other applicants to the swimming pool at OCS to take a mechanical aptitude test. We were given Scuba gear and a blacked out facemask. We were sent to the bottom of the pool with a bag full of pipefittings that we had to assemble within a set time without being able to see anything. The test was designed to measure your aptitude for working underwater and under pressure in low visibility conditions. I was not mechanically inclined. Growing in an apartment in the Bronx, the "super" who lived in the basement of the building did all the apartment repairs. At least I was at home in a swimming pool and was allowed to wear a bathing suit. In any case, I had no problem and successfully completed the task within the required time. I then filled out all the necessary paperwork to formally apply.

A week or so later, I was sent over to the destroyer piers at the Navy base at Newport, Rhode Island. There I was dressed out in the full gear of a Navy deep-sea diver. The helmet was extremely heavy and provided only a small window to see out. After being dressed in this gear, they had me pose for a souvenir Polaroid photo that I still have. I was then hoisted up and lowered into the cold, dark waters of Narragansett Bay. An air hose to the surface enabled me to breath underwater. This was actually a claustrophobia test to see how you would react to being totally confined in this suit and placed in the water with zero visibility. I had no problem with this particular test, either. For me, the entire experience was exciting and unforgettable.

Several weeks later, I was officially notified of my acceptance into the Navy EOD program and ordered to report to Underwater Swimmers School in Key West, Florida, on March 24, 1967, after my graduation from OCS. I sold my 1964 Volkswagen bug so I could buy an engagement ring and, on Christmas Day 1966, Kathy and I got engaged. OCS was a grueling ordeal for me – reveille at 5:00 am, spit-shining my "boonies," morning inspections, marching everywhere in formation, rigorous academic classes, limited study time, and little free time. Had it just been me, I never would have made it. But I wanted to get married and did not want to disappoint Kathy. On March 10, 1967, I completed OCS with distinction and was commissioned an Ensign in the United States Navy Reserve.

My future wife Kathy, her parents, and my mother were understandably not thrilled about my volunteering to work with live explosives and bombs. To them, and most others, this seemed like a dangerous and risky thing to do. I knew this was a volunteer program, from which I could opt out if I came to believe it was too dangerous. At the time, none of us knew that the danger was somewhat mitigated by the fact that the most common EOD "render safe procedure" (RSP) was not to manually dismantle an explosive device but to, in a variety of ways, "blow it in place" (BIP).

After a plane ride from New York City, followed by a bus ride from Miami down the Florida Keys, I arrived in Key West, Florida, to become a Navy diver. At the Underwater Swimmers School, I was qualified to use a variety of underwater breathing apparatus, including one that emitted few bubbles to avoid setting off acoustic underwater mines and one made of aluminum to avoid setting off magnetic underwater mines. When not under the water, we studied diving physics in the classroom and took long runs on the beach. After completing Underwater Swimmers School, I transferred to the Chemical and Biological Warfare School at Fort McClellan in Anniston, Alabama. There, I learned to render safe chemical and biological weapons while wearing a gas mask and a sealed butyl (or as we called it "brutal") rubber suit in 100-degree heat. As a souvenir of this training, I still have the scar on my forearm from the mustard gas drop deliberately left untreated to prove the ointment used to treat the drop placed next to it did, in fact, work.

After completing this part of the EOD training, I married Kathy on June 10, 1967, wearing my dress white Navy uniform. The ceremony was held back at St. Nicholas of Tolentine Church in the Bronx. It was the same church in which we had each received the sacraments of Baptism, Holy Communion, and Confirmation in our Catholic faith. Father Sofranko, the priest who presided over our wedding, was also my former high school biology teacher. Several times during the wedding ceremony, I smiled as my mind wandered back to those classes when he would humorously remind us that the penis was an organ, not a muscle, and did not need to be exercised. It was his way of using humor to remind us to avoid what our religion called the "occasion of sin."

The next day, Sunday, my new bride and I drove to beautiful downtown Indian Head, Maryland, so I could start the last phase of my training at the EOD School at the Naval Ordnance Station located there. When we arrived, we were assigned to a Navy housing apartment that was considered substandard and not what Kathy was expecting, based on photos I had shown her of the Navy housing in Key West, Florida. As a former New Yorker who had spent many a late night searching for street parking in the Bronx, I was thrilled just to have an assigned parking space. Because I was a temporary student resident, our housing building had both officers and enlisted personnel living in it. A Chief Petty Officer living upstairs had six children.

There was some culture shock for a young couple from the Bronx. One day, the mailman told my wife she talked like Mugsy from "The Bowery Boys" movies. We played the legal slot machines in Charles County, Maryland when doing our laundry at the local laundromat. Still, we were newlyweds and made the best of it, knowing we would have limited time together during this last phase of my EOD training. We never got to have a real honeymoon, but we were able to get some "exercise" in honor of Father Sofranko. On Monday morning, I reported for my first class at the EOD School.

I didn't realize it then, but I had taken another fork in life's road that would eventually lead me to becoming the FBI's leading expert on child sexual victimization. Of course, at the time, I had no idea. All I know was that I was in love and "I wanted to get married." I had volunteered for an important Navy program for dubious reasons – because it would allow me to be with my new wife for at least a few months. Granted, this wasn't the best reason to volunteer to handle explosives and bombs during a war. I didn't really know what I was getting into, but my desire to get married had set into motion a series of events that would alter the direction of my professional and personal life.

The remaining six months of my EOD training at Indian Head, Maryland, went by fairly quickly. All branches of service sent their EOD personnel to this same school, but the training for Navy personnel was the longest because only they were trained in rendering safe underwater weapons, munitions, and devices. There was a big difference between diving in the warm, blue waters of Key West, Florida and diving in the cold, black waters of the Potomac River in Maryland. Practical exercises at nearby Stump Neck, Maryland and at Eglin Air Force Base in Florida involved learning to handle live explosives. It was hard work and I had to study long hours for the many examinations we were given. But each night I went home to my new wife, which, at the time, was the biggest blessing of my life. That would soon change, though, because a few months after arriving, Kathy became pregnant. Our baby was due in May 1968.

Of the members of my EOD class, six were, like me, brand new ensigns right out of OCS and the other fifteen were enlisted men with varying years of Navy experience; including one who was a Navy SEAL. As our training came to a close, our post-graduation duty assignments became the primary center of our attention. For the six officers in the class, the Bureau of Navy Personnel sent down six sets of orders with no names on them. The officer with the highest class standing would pick first, then the officer ranked second would choose, and so on. When the officer orders finally arrived in December 1967, they essentially consisted of five sets of orders likely leading to duty in Vietnam and one set of orders to stay at the EOD School in Indian Head to be an instructor. Since I held the top ranking in my class, I chose first. Because I was newly married with my first child to be born in a few months, the choice was obvious to me.

My firstborn, a daughter we named Melissa Jane, was born in May 1968 at Bethesda Naval Hospital. I spent the next two years and three months assigned as an instructor at the EOD School in Indian Head. I also had many collateral duties as Supply Officer, Personnel Officer, and Range Safety Officer. As Range Safety Officer I had to supervise many practical problems for trainees that involved use of live explosives. One of my duties was to return to Navy OCS in Newport, Rhode Island, and give the same presentation and administer the same screening tests to EOD applicants I had received. In 2008, after retiring from the FBI, I again had an opportunity to return to Navy OCS while doing a presentation on "Cyber Sex Offenders" at the U.S. Naval Justice School located a short distance away. While there, I discovered that Nimitz Hall, the brand new OCS dormitory facility I had lived in for five months back in 1966-67, was being renovated. In 2016, the new FBI Academy, that I first attended in 1972 shortly after it opened, was also being renovated. Such work made me feel old and in need of some rehab myself.

I enjoyed my new job at the EOD School, but whatever my duties, the best part was I could continue to go home almost every night to my new family. I understood that I was a very lucky man, particularly during a war. I personally knew several outstanding EOD men who went to Vietnam and never came home. I sometimes felt guilty about my assignment and I thanked God every day for my good fortune. It is a little embarrassing, though, to tell people I was in the Navy for over three years and yet I had never deployed on a ship.

The EOD School was a Navy school with a Navy officer as the Commanding Officer. Because all branches of the military sent their EOD personnel to this same School, the staff consisted of officers and enlisted personnel from all branches of service. Therefore, although I was in the Navy for more than three years, I never developed a strong identification with only the Navy. I worked with and learned to appreciate the contributions of all branches of the U.S. military. I worked with some Marine Corps personnel who were attempting to arrange for the use of the explosive ranges at the Quantico Marine Corps Base in Virginia for parts of the EOD basic training program. The Quantico Marine Corps Base was almost directly across the Potomac River from the EOD School in Indian Head, Maryland. At the time, I had no idea how significant that early time spent so close to and associated with Quantico, Virginia, would later become in my professional life.

My decision to join the military was one of the smartest things I ever did. Much of what I accomplished later in life was built on the foundation of my military service. In addition, in the years that followed my military service I used my veterans benefits to purchase my first home in San Antonio, Texas with no money down and pay for graduate school in Texas and California. Although I thoroughly appreciated my time in the Navy, I didn't intend to make it my career. Since my college days, I had dreamed about being an FBI Special Agent (SA). My best friend's father had been an FBI agent and James Stewart as SA Chip Hardesty in *The FBI Story* movie and Efrem Zimbalist, Jr. as Inspector Erskine in *The F.B.I.* TV program both influenced me. When I was ten years old I was even the president of a junior FBI agents club we formed in my neighborhood. In college, I majored in accounting with just that goal in mind. My superior officers at the EOD School were well aware of that interest. As my three-year obligation of active duty service to the Navy was coming to a close, my Executive Officer (XO) introduced me to two FBI agents, Fred Smith and Chuck Killion, who regularly came to the EOD School. These agents were assigned to the Explosives Unit at the FBI Laboratory at FBI Headquarters in Washington, DC. Due to my military background in explosives, they wanted to recruit me into the FBI. Because I didn't have any post-college accounting experience to go with my degree, I didn't qualify under the FBI's Accounting Program. However, with my three years experience as a Navy officer, I did qualify under a separate Modified Program.

These two agents helped me apply to the FBI and arranged the necessary tests and interviews. But, during my actual FBI interview, the agent conducting it seemed to have little interest in my explosives background or my military security clearances. He told me all of that would be behind me if I became an FBI Special Agent. I wasn't sure if that meant he thought I was a good candidate or not. I was about to leave the Navy, but the FBI had not yet accepted me. I had a wife and child, but soon I would have no job or income.

As the end of my Navy career approached, I became increasingly worried. Then I received a phone call from the Applicant Unit at FBI Headquarters. Because of my degree in Accounting, the agent wanted to know if I would be willing to take a specialized accounting test after completing FBI New Agent training to also qualify under the Accounting Program. Since I had not done any accounting work in several years, I told him I was willing if I had time to refresh my knowledge. He said fine and told me to call him if I didn't have a new agent appointment letter in the next few days. I soon received the letter dated February 13, 1970 offering me a probationary appointment as an FBI Special Agent at a starting salary of $10,252 per year. If I chose to accept the appointment, I was instructed to report to Washington, DC, on May 4, 1970.

I was thrilled; knowing my dream of becoming an FBI agent was about to be fulfilled. In March 1970, I was released from active duty in the Navy as a full Lieutenant and assigned to the Standby Reserve. I assumed that my involvement with explosives and being a training instructor was over. Leaving Indian Head, Maryland, I drove Kathy and our young daughter back to the Bronx, where we would live with my mother. They would remain there while I reported to and completed FBI New Agent training in Washington, DC.

I couldn't wait to see where the next fork in life's road would take me.

CHAPTER TWO

"Don't Worry, It Will Never Happen"

On May 4, 1970, I reported to the Old Post Office Building (now occupied by the Trump International Hotel) on Pennsylvania Avenue in Washington, DC, to begin my sixteen weeks of New Agent training with the FBI. I was part of "NAC 16" (New Agent Class number sixteen of that year). Preoccupied with the start of my career with the FBI, I took little note that on that very day National Guard troops shot and killed four anti war protesting students at Kent State University in Ohio.

Back then, most of the training for FBI new agents took place in Washington, DC. New agents had to find their own housing in the DC area and commute to class each day at the Old Post Office Building. I had my car with me and after class on Fridays I drove to the Bronx to see my wife and family for the weekend. At this time, new agents went to the FBI Academy at Quantico, Virginia, only for a few weeks at the beginning of the training and another week towards the end. The FBI Academy then consisted of one relatively small multi-purpose building and firing ranges on the Marine Corps Base. Agents slept eight to a room and used a common bathroom down the hall. While at Quantico, I observed veteran FBI agents coming back to the FBI Academy for what was called In-Service Training. As I understood it then, these were usually one- or two-week classes for experienced agents focusing on a specialized or advanced investigative topic.

I thought I did well in my New Agent training, but I didn't discover how well until later on. My class counselor was impressed when I was the only member of my class who could recite the preamble to the U.S. Constitution, which begins "We the People of the United States, in Order to form a more perfect Union, establish Justice..." My solid Catholic education served me well. I had no problem with the academic subjects and the regular written examination. Firearms training was another matter. I had never owned or fired a gun in my life. Even in the Navy, I handled improvised explosive devices but never fired a gun. This eventually turned out to be an advantage because I had no bad habits and learned to shoot the Bureau way. Unlike many new agents from New York City, I did at least have a driver's license. One day during my training, my class counselor asked if I was ready to take the FBI accounting test I had agreed to take before getting my appointment letter. I embarrassingly told him that I had not yet had any time to study for it. He told me to forget about it. I was already an FBI agent and they couldn't now make me take it. Although I would not be a Special Agent Accountant, my decision to major in Accounting had not been in vain – it got me in the door.

As New Agent training neared its end, I learned that my first office of assignment in the FBI would be St. Louis, Missouri. Also around this time in the sixteen-week training, new agents were assigned to work with a veteran FBI agent in the Washington Field Office in Washington, DC. I was his (no female agents then) partner for one week and got to see what it was like to be a working FBI Special Agent on the streets in the real world. It was some of the best training I received. One day during this week, my temporary veteran partner told me that I had a message to go see Supervisory Special Agent (SSA) Jack Kirsch. SSA Kirsch had an office one floor up in the same Old Post Office Building where most of my new agent classes were being held.

I reported to his office as quickly as I could. I had no idea why an FBI Supervisor assigned to FBI Headquarters would want to see me, a lowly new agent in training. I came to know and admire Jack Kirsch very well. However, to communicate the awe I felt about him at the time of this summons, I will refer to him here by his official title – SSA Kirsch. When I first met SSA Kirsch I was impressed with the fact that he seemed to treat me as a fellow FBI agent and not as a new agent trainee. He explained that he worked in a special planning office that developed new and innovative programs for the FBI. One of his big jobs was developing training programs and the academic curriculum for the new FBI Academy complex that was being built at the Marine Corps Base at Quantico, Virginia. He introduced me to his coworkers, most of whom had advanced academic degrees in various areas. Many of these individuals would become Unit Chiefs and faculty members at the new FBI Academy when it opened in 1972. Their work seemed very impressive, and I was proud that there were such agents in the FBI.

I still did not know why I was being called to his office. SSA Kirsch eventually explained that the FBI and American law enforcement were currently facing growing problems with new-left radicals using bombs and improvised explosive devices as part of their violent protests against the government. He was developing an In-Service Training program on "bombing matters" to help address this problem. He then verified with me that while in the Navy I had been an instructor at the Explosive Ordnance Disposal (EOD) School in Indian Head, Maryland. I knew this fact had to be in my FBI personnel file, but I didn't understand how he would have readily known this. He went on to explain that this two-week In-Service Training on Bombing Matters would be held at the current FBI Academy building at Quantico, Virginia. He explained that this advanced training was scheduled to start on the Monday following the completion of my New Agent training on a Wednesday. He then concluded by asking if I would like to volunteer to be a member of this special training class and add my expertise to the program. If I agreed, he would then get final approval from his superiors and the Director – **J. Edgar Hoover** himself.

I was flabbergasted and overwhelmed. I desperately wanted him to be impressed by my knowledge and professional skills. How could I tell him that I really did not fully understand what he was telling and asking me? I quickly thought of the stalling tactic of telling him that I was very interested, but I had to discuss it with my wife. He had no problem with that but asked me to get back to him as quickly as possible. Although I would discuss this with my wife, the person I really needed to get to was my New Agent Class Counselor – William Beane.

After many weeks of New Agent training, I had come to respect and rely on SA Beane. He had been an FBI street agent for almost 20 years and seemed to understand every aspect of the FBI. I located him as quickly as I could. I told him about my meeting with SSA Kirsch and what he wanted me to do. I asked if he had any advice. He grinned and said this was an easy situation to resolve. He went on to explain that if I said no to SSA Kirsch, it would not look good. As a new FBI agent, I should be enthusiastic and want to help the Bureau any way I could. Therefore, it was important that I tell SSA Kirsch that I would volunteer to participate in this important new In-Service Training. But then he went on to explain that it really did not matter. He said he had been in the FBI for 20 years and knew how it operated. He said SSA Kirsch might be a creative and innovative agent, but there was no way the FBI would ever allow a brand new agent who had never worked in a field office to go to In-Service Training. Such training was only for experienced field agents. SSA Kirsch might want to do this, but it will never be approved by the powers that be. He told me, *"don't worry, it will never happen."*

I returned to SSA Kirsch's office the next day and enthusiastically told him that I wanted to be part of his specialized training program. I left his office believing that my FBI career was off to a good start. I had been noticed for my special expertise and had impressed my superiors with my can-do spirit, but I would not have to worry about the unknown implications of this bombing training. I would soon be reporting to my first office to begin learning how to be an FBI street agent. I went back to focusing on my remaining New Agent training. A few days later, I was told to report back to SSA Kirsch's office. I assumed I was going to hear his explanation for why I would not be going to the training. I was prepared to accept my rejection with some feigned disappointment. As I walked into his office, SSA Kirsch had a big smile on his face. He proudly announced that I would be going to the In-Service Training. He informed me that Director Hoover himself had approved the request memorandum by putting his "H" on it in the blue ink that only he was allowed to use. I was shocked and surprised but tried to pretend that I was excited and pleased.

Attempting to maintain my composure, I struggled to calmly ask what would happen next. SSA Kirsch seemed thrilled and satisfied. He explained that he would begin working out the details. He would let me know everything I needed to know and do. The end result was that I became the first, and as far as I know the only, FBI agent ever to go to Advanced In-Service Training right out of New Agent training. Years later in the book and movie *Silence of the Lambs*, the character of SA Clarice Starling would work cases in the field without even completing New Agent training. But that was the movies; this was the real world. Although surprised by the decision, I became enthusiastic that I would now be utilizing my military training to help the FBI investigate bombing cases. This was another unexpected fork in the road of my life.

I graduated from New Agent training on Wednesday, August 12, 1970, and reported to SSA Kirsch's office on the next morning. Because the In-Service training would not start until the following Monday, it was decided that I would become a kind of temporary Bureau Supervisor in the FBI Training Division for two days. So I worked with SSA Jack Kirsch and his partner SSA Marty McNerney to help finalize the training that I would soon be attending. Essentially, this made me something of an anomaly within the FBI: I was a Bureau Supervisor before I was ever a field agent.

On Monday, August 17, 1970, approximately sixty veteran FBI agents and one brand new one reported to the old FBI Academy in Quantico, Virginia, to begin the training. There was one agent from each FBI field office (fifty-nine) and two extra agents – a former Army EOD Officer still in his first office of assignment and myself. As I settled in for the training I was soon surprised by something I noticed in the handout material I was provided. The schedule page indicated that the official title of this class was *Advanced Police Instructors' In-Service on Bombings and Bomb Threats*. What was a basic police instructor and why was this class called advanced? After repeated discussions about lesson plans and training aids, I gradually came to realize that this class was more about the FBI training local law enforcement about bombing matters than about the FBI actually investigating bombing cases. I learned that I was about to become something the FBI called a *Police*

Instructor in bombing matters. Talking to my classmates, I found out that the FBI does a lot of training for state and local law enforcement around the country. This was an aspect of FBI work I was not familiar with and had not anticipated. I thought, however, that this might be an interesting part of my new career. I had been an instructor at the EOD School.

Then one day in the middle of this training, Jack Kirsch came in and announced to the class that he had gotten permission to also designate every agent attending as a *General Police Instructor* (GPI). What was that? On the next break, I quietly approached Jack Kirsch and asked what it meant to be a GPI. He explained that as a GPI, I would be considered qualified to teach not only bombing but also every general topic the FBI then taught. I told Jack Kirsch that I thought I might be able to teach bombing matters because of my military background, but doubted my ability to teach other law enforcement topics. I still had not even investigated a single case. I didn't yet know how to be a regular FBI agent. He said he understood and that I shouldn't worry because there was the other experienced agent in the class from the St. Louis Division to which I was being transferred. This other agent would do all the bombing training in my new office. I would just monitor his presentations for at least a year. He said there were other experienced police instructors in the St. Louis Division who would teach the other topics. He stated he primarily wanted me in this class so that I could share my specialized knowledge of explosives with the other agents attending.

I felt relieved and settled in to participate and learn as much as I could. It was a great experience to interact with all these veteran agents and learn what the FBI was really all about. Soon I was informed that the agent who was in charge of the FBI field police training program had decided that he did not want me designated as a police instructor at all because of my inexperience. This was fine with me. I was still not sure exactly what it meant to be a police instructor. This might be something I could do later in my career.

After completing the two-week In-Service, I reported to my first office in St. Louis. I found an apartment for my family to live, joined a car pool with other agents living in my neighborhood while my wife learned to drive, and started working my newly assigned cases. However, after just a few days, the veteran agent from the St. Louis office who had attended the Bombing In-Service with me told me that he was soon being transferred. I had been told that I would just be monitoring his presentations and now I learned he would not even be around. I also learned that one of the reasons for the In-service I attended was because the FBI Annual Law Enforcement Conferences for 1970 would be on the topic of bombing. The Special Agent in Charge (SAC) and police instructors from the St. Louis FBI field office were scheduled to travel all over the office territory in Eastern Missouri doing presentations on this topic. The SAC decided I was now the most qualified person to do, and therefore should do, these presentations. The SAC wrote a communication to FBI Headquarters requesting that they authorize my use as a police instructor in bombing matters only. The Training Division responded, stating that they "ordinarily would never recommend the approval of a first-office Agent as a police instructor; however, in this instance we are dealing with a highly specialized subject matter which requires instructors with background knowledge regarding explosives." With the stipulation that my appearances as a police instructor be restricted to bombing schools, they approved my participation in training schools when I was needed.

With that, my career as an FBI field police instructor began. I was a police instructor almost from my first day in my first office. I spent the next year teaching bombing matters all over Eastern Missouri. In addition, during that year there were a series of terrorist bombings by new-left radicals against government facilities in the area. It was decided that my bombing expertise would also be used during FBI investigations. I was dispatched by my supervisors to process several bombing crime scenes, including one at the U.S. Civilian Personnel Record Center. It turned out this bombing was mostly a diversion secondary device to set up two larger bombings later that day to kill first responders. I likewise responded to those after they detonated. I also assisted other agents in interviews of

suspects in these bombing cases. My bosses seemed happy with my
work in this area. In July 1971, I received my transfer to San Antonio,
Texas, as my second office. At this time, FBI agents were assigned to
their first office for almost exactly one year and then transferred to
another office. In theory this was to give you a fresh start after all the
mistakes that first office agents typically make.

San Antonio, Texas, was a great place to live and raise a family
for the next seven years. My second child, a baby boy we named
Richard, was born there. Based on the number of agents assigned,
the office was then relatively small. However, it covered a very large
geographical area that included most of central Texas all the way
down to the Rio Grande Valley and the border with Mexico. Each
workday I walked through the grounds of the historic Alamo to get
from the FBI office to where my Bureau car was parked. During my
time there, I was assigned to several different squads and worked a
wide variety of cases. This included surveilling Soviet agents into
pornographic movie theaters and babysitting Mafia leader Sam
Giancana during his brief stopover in San Antonio – on his way to
Chicago after being deported from Mexico. I was assigned domestic
security cases involving subversive individuals and other groups
advocating violent overthrow of the government. To encourage
dissension, the Soviet Union was meddling in the antiwar and civil
rights movements. The FBI was trying to determine the extent. For
complicated administrative reasons, for a time I was assigned all the
Weather Underground and new left radical cases in the San Antonio
Division. These terrorists decided that the best way to protest war
was to blow things up and hurt people. Although long forgotten
today by most Americans, their names (Bill Ayers, Bernardine Dohrn,
Katherine Ann Power, Susan Saxe, Dwight Alan Armstrong, David
Sylvan Fine), their crimes, and their images on FBI Fugitive posters
still resonate in my brain. I will let their admitted behavior speak for
itself and not apologize for FBI efforts to stop them based on 20/20
hindsight.

My squad supervisor was my immediate superior and assigned
my investigative work. Another agent, however, coordinated the

police training program and was not technically my supervisor. He assigned only my training work. It was like working for two bosses at the same time. The training coordinator agent quickly learned about my having been designated a police instructor in bombing matters while assigned to the St. Louis office. Since I had far more experience than the agent from San Antonio who had been in the bombing In-Service with me, he wanted me to do more such training for the police in the San Antonio Division.

However, my squad supervisor was not a big fan of the FBI police training program and discouraged me from doing it. I was torn; my supervisor acted as if I was on vacation during the time I spent conducting training away from my real job as an investigative agent. In actuality, the days I spent instructing were some of the most physically and mentally exhausting days of my FBI career.

Although investigation was clearly its primary job, the FBI could not do that job effectively without the cooperation of state and local law enforcement. The FBI police training program was the best police liaison program the FBI had, and it was free – one program where it clearly could not be claimed that the FBI took from the locals and gave nothing in return. The only FBI agents whom most state and local law enforcement officers ever meet are the agents who provide them with this training. From the 1930s through the 1970s this was a major, if not the only, source of training for many local law enforcement officers in the United States. I came to strongly believe in this program for the police and the liaison return benefit for the FBI.

As I taught more and more bombing schools and responded to a few bombing crime scene investigations, the response was extremely positive. In 1973, the training coordinator came to me to ask if I would now like to teach a topic other than bombing. I asked what else I could teach. I had learned about bombs and explosives in the military. He said not to worry. The FBI would provide me with the training I needed to teach. Just like the In-Service I had attended on bombing matters, I would be sent to a specialized school on a specific police training topic. He provided me with a list of topics and dates for the specialized training. As I went down through the list I saw topics such as *Defensive Tactics, Firearms, Fingerprints, Organized Crime,* and *Photography.* Nothing I saw really appealed to me until near the bottom of the page. There I saw the magical three-letter word *S-E-X* followed by the word *Crimes.* You mean I can go to In-Service Training where the FBI will teach me about sex? He said there was such training. Intrigued about the topic but for all the wrong reasons, I then volunteered to attend this *Sex Crimes* training. Little did I know what importance that training held for me.

In November 1973, I attended a two-week *Sex Crimes Investigation Instructors' School.* This training was held at the new and greatly expanded FBI Academy complex in Quantico, Virginia, that was now completed and open. Walter McLaughlin, an agent assigned to the Philadelphia FBI Office, began the FBI's training program in what it called *Sex Crimes* back in the 1960s. I am not sure how he developed his expertise in this area. His training classes on the topic eventually became so popular that FBIHQ asked him to come to Quantico to train other FBI agents from around the country to teach these classes – a train-the-trainer class. An agent named Frank Sass, who had been trained by Walter McLaughlin, organized and put on the school I attended. SSA Sass was an instructor assigned to the new Behavioral Science Unit (BSU) at Quantico.

Just prior to going to this sex crimes training, I was sent to another In-Service for *Special Weapons and Tactics* (SWAT) training. Also attending this SWAT class was an agent from another field office who had also been trained as an instructor in sex crimes by SA McLaughlin. When I told him I would soon be going to this training myself, he said this was one of the best topics to teach. He told me that if I followed three recommendations I could not go wrong. His recommendations were: (1) Show lots of pornography to the class, (2) Have a wide variety of dirty jokes to go with each perverted sexual activity I was discussing, and (3) Allow no women in the class – because he said, if there were woman in the class you could not implement the first two recommendations. This was obviously an agent whose time had passed. I never followed his advice. Since

I began teaching this topic in 1973, I cannot recall a single class in which there were no women. But I have taught many classes in which there were no men.

The FBI *Sex Crimes* training I received was very good, but I soon recognized that this was a very complex subject matter. I had gone to sex crimes training believing I would be learning more about sex. I quickly realized that the emphasis was in fact on the crimes and not the sex. What I was taught by the FBI was substantial, but clearly just a beginning. I became fascinated and intrigued by the whole issue of human behavior and its motivation. If I were going to teach this topic effectively, I knew I had to learn a lot more about it. When I returned to San Antonio, I began to learn everything I could about sex crimes and deviant sexual behavior. I read books, talked to and consulted with the local police sex crimes investigators, and enrolled in graduate school at Sam Houston State University. This was a criminal justice program with a strong emphasis on psychology. I started teaching classes on sex crimes investigation to local law enforcement; eventually, more than on bombing because after the Vietnam War ended, bombings by the radical left terrorists pretty much stopped. Of course, many years later there would be an increase in bombings by the radical right. In March 1978, I was transferred from the FBI field office in San Antonio, Texas to the one in Los Angeles, California.

While a street or field agent from 1970 to 1980, I received FBI In-Service and specialized training at Quantico over 25 times. I went to numerous additional advanced training schools on bombing and arson matters. This included graduating from the Hazardous Devices School at Redstone Arsenal, Alabama, in 1974 after which I became one of the first FBI agents certified as a bomb technician authorized to handle live explosives during training schools. After that, I was re-certified at specialized seminars held annually at the FBI Academy. As a field agent, I served as a certified FBI "bomb tech" in the San Antonio and Los Angeles offices.

I also attended additional advanced trainings on *Sex Crimes* and *Sexual Exploitation of Children*. I became a certified police instructor in the areas of *Hostage Negotiation* and *Crime Resistance*. I graduated from the Texas Crime Prevention Institute. I completed FBI training in *Special Weapons and Tactics* (SWAT). I completed 75 graduate credits in two University Masters Programs. Most of the training schools I conducted in the field were on the topics of *Bombing*, *Sex Crimes*, and *Hostage Negotiation*. These were three intrinsically interesting topics. For these ten years, I also continued to function primarily as an investigative agent assigned cases by my squad supervisor.

While assigned to the Los Angeles FBI office, I became increasingly frustrated with this dual career. I enjoyed conducting training and I enjoyed investigating cases, but it was getting harder and harder to do both. Many of my investigative supervisors discouraged and sometimes even penalized me for doing training. I had two bosses, but only one of them did my annual performance appraisal. I finally decided that I would either become a full-time police instructor or stop doing it. Within the FBI, the easiest way to become a full-time instructor is to be assigned to the Training Division at the FBI Academy in Quantico, Virginia. But first you had to have at least a Masters Degree, which I eventually obtained. During the summer of 1979, I also volunteered and spent three months at the FBI Academy on temporary assignment as a counselor for the 118th Session of the FBI National Academy.

Many people are confused by or interchangeably use the terms *FBI Academy* and *FBI National Academy*. The FBI Academy is a large complex of buildings and facilities located on 385 acres within the Marine Corps Base at Quantico. It is like a college campus. The FBI National Academy (NA) is not a place, but a ten-week training program for law enforcement conducted by the FBI at the FBI Academy. The opportunity to be an NA counselor was a kind of "try before you buy" opportunity to find out what it would be like to be assigned to the FBI Academy without making a permanent commitment. While there in 1979, I attended as many classes as I could that the Behavioral Science Unit (BSU) conducted. If I were transferred to the FBI Academy, I hoped to be assigned to this Unit.

I increasingly became interested in behavioral science subjects. The topics I was teaching such as Sex Crimes, Hostage Negotiations, Criminal Psychology, and Crime Resistance were or began under the BSU's umbrella. I made sure the BSU Unit Chief, Larry Monroe, personally knew about me and my training and experience in these areas. It turned out that this Unit Chief's grandmother had worked at the rectory at my former Catholic parish in the Bronx.

When I returned to Los Angeles, I told Kathy what I had observed and learned during my time as an NA counselor. It seemed that being assigned to Quantico would be a great job in every way. I already had ten years under my belt as a field investigator. I would be able to focus my efforts on conducting training and be evaluated based only on that. I finally finished my Master's Degree in May of 1980 and advised the Training Division of my status and interest. I enjoyed working in the glitz of the Los Angeles area and loved living in Thousand Oaks in Ventura County, where I could afford a home. However, I increasingly came to hate the long, traffic-congested commute each day to get to and from where I lived and worked.

Around this time, I also requested to see a copy of my newly available FBI personnel file. When I got it, the most noteworthy thing I found was the communication that SSA Jack Kirsch had written in July 1970 to get approval for my attendance at that first bombing In-Service. Among the details of my qualifications and accomplishments, the memorandum states that I was the academic leader of my New Agent Class with an average grade of ninety-nine percent. This was surprising to me because we had repeatedly been told that there were no class standings for New Agent training. We had been told that you either graduated or you did not. Reading this communication, I gained a better appreciation of the importance of a record of excellence. It also mentioned my honor grades in college and graduating with distinction from OCS and at the head of my class in EOD training. Things that I had long since forgotten about might have played a significant role in how I got to where I was and where I was going. Things done for other reasons wound up having unintended or unimagined consequences. I realized that whatever you do, doing your best could be rewarding on many levels.

In December 1980, I finally received orders transferring me to a supervisory position in the Training Division at FBI Headquarters (the same position I had temporarily filled for two days after I graduated from New Agent training in 1970)! I would now be a real Supervisory Special Agent (SSA) in the BSU in Quantico. I wondered what SSA Jack Kirsch, who had started me on my journey, would have thought about all of this. By that time, Jack had retired from the FBI after serving as the first BSU Unit Chief after the new FBI Academy opened in 1972. Ten years after working with him at the Old Post Office Building, I would now be working in the Unit he had help create and first headed.

The FBI named, renamed, and expanded the BSU many times over the years. The only names that have stuck are those made famous by *Silence of the Lambs* (BSU) and more recently by *Criminal Minds* (Behavioral Analysis Unit or BAU). The five current BAUs are no longer even part of the Training Division. They are part of the FBI Critical Incident Response Group (CIRG) in Stafford, Virginia, and the amount of training they do is greatly reduced from the original BSU. This book is not the place to attempt to explain why this was done and what each of these Units now do. Whatever the name, my work remained essentially the same for the next twenty years I was assigned there. Therefore, for purposes of this book, I will use the commonly known term *Behavioral Science Unit* when referring to the Unit where I worked all those years. Because I was assigned in this Unit from 1980 to 2000, I eventually became a kind of bridge from the old BSU to the new BAU.

During the first decade of my assignment to the BSU, I continued to re-certify as a bomb tech at the annual Advanced Explosives Recertification Seminar held at the Academy. By the late 1980s, however, I realized I couldn't maintain my proficiency in bombing matters and pursue my new work in BSU. I eventually allowed my certification to lapse and the significant "bombs" phase of my journey pretty much ended.

My assignment to the BSU in 1980 was another major fork in the road on a journey that would change my life in ways I never could have imagined. Because of the publicity this Unit has received over the years, fueled by books, movies, and TV programs, I have been asked many times by young people about the best way to someday be assigned to the Behavioral Science Unit. They often ask for guidance about the best choice for an appropriate major in college. I usually tell them an abbreviated version of my story, and then surprise them with my seemingly irrelevant major in – Accounting!

CHAPTER THREE

"Land of the Giants"

When I showed up to work in the FBI Behavioral Science Unit (BSU), I felt like I had entered the *Land of the Giants*. The Unit's mission, of training and education, began in 1972. It was one of several academic training Units created at the newly built and expanded FBI Academy. Through the efforts of some creative and innovative agents assigned to it, the Unit (part of a Training Division) also became involved in doing research and consulting on active and cold investigations. Eventually, the BSU's most famous work evolved into providing investigative assistance to criminal justice professionals in the United States and foreign countries. This type of operational or consulting casework became popularly known as *profiling*. The concept soon became so trendy that a feature story in the April 1983 issue of *Psychology Today* magazine, complete with a group centerfold photograph, referred to that Unit as the "Mind Hunters."

Many administrators within the FBI and its Training Division didn't support this expansion into non-training areas, so the history of the BSU is the story of what a group of dedicated, intelligent, self-motivated, overachieving, and egotistical agents were able to achieve in spite of an upper management that often did not understand, care about, or agree with what the agents were doing. I came to realize that it's the simultaneous involvement in training, research, and case consultation that produces the highest level of knowledge and expertise in any area. Instead of trying to curtail these expansion efforts by the BSU, the administrators of the Training Division should have encouraged all the other academic training Units to do the same.

When I arrived in 1981, this expansion was still in its early stages. The BSU's research and case consultation components emerged during the late 1970s and early 1980s with no real clear plan or even approval from the Training Division's heads. In the mid-1970s, BSU agents like Pat Mullaney and Howard Tetan pioneered the early involvement into operational work. It began informally, by applying what was known about criminal behavior from solved and closed cases to unsolved and pending cases. This often occurred in the classroom during presentations to law enforcement officers attending the FBI National Academy program or other FBI training programs. Mullaney soon got involved in ongoing kidnapping and hostage negotiation cases. I got to know "Tetan and Mullaney," as they became known, from some of the FBI In-Service training I attended before being assigned to the BSU. In addition to their early application of behavioral analysis to operational casework, they also perfected the art of team teaching. Alone, each was a great instructor; together they were a finely tuned machine. The very first time I heard Pat Mullaney and his familiar New York accent, I thought he seemed familiar. When I spoke to him, he told me he used to teach at Manhattan Prep in the Bronx, NY during the 1960s, when he was a Christian Brother. Manhattan Prep was in the same building at Manhattan College where I took many of my undergraduate classes. I had probably passed him many times in the hallways. Sadly, Pat Mullaney, one of the true pioneers of the BSU, passed away in 2017.

By the late 1970s, innovative BSU agents like John Douglas, Bob Ressler, and Roy Hazelwood were expanding and refining this operational casework specifically into the areas of serial killing and rape. Part of the BSU's varied training mission was to conduct one-week *road schools* (usually by two BSU agents) for state and local police throughout the country. These schools were usually conducted in between each of the four sessions per year of the FBI National Academy program. While out on these *road schools*, BSU members began doing research by going into prisons to interview convicted and notorious murderers, serial killers, sex offenders, and assassins. The original intended purpose was not strictly research. The agents were also hoping to increase their credibility with the officers attending their classes. They soon realized how much valuable information they were learning from this evolving research. The cases of those being interviewed were adjudicated and their convictions upheld. These were research, not investigative, interviews. Some accused the BSU of conducting sham research interviews to surreptitiously get investigative information. This wasn't true and indicated a lack of understanding of the evolving work of the Unit. Within the BSU, this research was eventually designated as the *Criminal Personality Research Project*.

Before conducting those interviews, agents meticulously studied all the details of the subjects' crimes. This reduced reliance on the offenders' self-reported information and was a distinguishing characteristic of early FBI research interviews. Self-serving versions of their crimes could be explored and then challenged. As a result, we learned much about the post-offense behavior of criminals and the **how** of their crimes. The value of such research interviews was soon recognized by and expanded with the support of the Office of Juvenile Justice and Delinquency Prevention (OJJDP) of the U.S. Department of Justice (*see* Lanning, 1995).

Other outstanding BSU agents such as Jim Reese (who also died in 2017), Bob Schaefer, and Dick Ault, were applying knowledge of the behavioral sciences to other important law enforcement interests such as stress management and espionage.

The agents in this Unit were some of the FBI's best and brightest. They were many of the agents who had trained me when, during the 1970s, I attended specialized In-Service and National Academy classes. Because they taught courses that were accredited by the University of Virginia, they all had advanced degrees. They were gifted presenters who could keep a group of experienced police officers captivated and interested while teaching them what they needed to know about criminal behavior. Those agents were my role models. I was now in the big leagues – but I was uncertain whether I could ever measure up to their standards.

As the junior member, I was at first assigned a wide range of miscellaneous jobs. I modified the BSU curriculum for and taught FBI new agents. I taught a short hostage negotiation class to the National Academy (NA). I filled in for other BSU instructors who were away teaching. As mentioned, members of the Unit traveled around the country in pairs teaching one-week *road schools* at state and local police facilities. When I began to do this, I was typically teamed with another more experienced BSU agent. I struggled to keep up, but I was an experienced instructor – and I now had access to training material and resources I had only dreamed about in the past.

The offices for the BSU agents were then located in the basement of the FBI Academy Library – called the *Learning Resource Center.* I certainly would have liked a private office, but each office was a good-sized open room with a wide entrance, and no door. Two agents were assigned to each office. Mine was across the hall from the office of John Douglas and Bob Ressler, two of the Unit's leaders in this expansion into research and case consultation. As a result, for several years I was able to regularly overhear their conversations with each other and with the growing number of investigators and prosecutors who frequently contacted them for advice and guidance. It was some of the best training I could have hoped for, to prepare me for the growing consulting work I would do.

Although this type of casework was and still is most often referred to as *profiling,* that is only a small part of what the Unit eventually did operationally. As the term is now used by the BSU, *profiling* is defined as a detailed description of the characteristics of an *unknown subject* ("unsub"). At the beginning, the concept of profiling was applied only to old, unsolved murder cases with no apparent motive and after all other investigative leads were exhausted. Over time, such consulting work evolved and expanded into a wide range of practical applications of the behavioral sciences (e.g., interview strategy, post-offense behavior, personality assessments, proactive strategies, victimology, prosecutive strategy, and expert search warrants) to the criminal justice system. Continued use of the term *profiling,* however, has become unfortunate and misleading. It has negative connotations for many people. Even now when I describe my work in the BSU, people almost always ask if I was a "profiler." I usually just say yes, because it does no good to try to explain otherwise. But today the FBI usually refers to this type of consulting casework as *Criminal Investigative Analysis* or *Behavioral Analysis*.

Sometime around late 1981, fellow BSU member Roy Hazelwood approached me. Roy was the Unit's expert in what was initially, and at the time of my 1973 in-service training, referred to as *Sex Crimes*. One of Roy's great accomplishments was changing this area from a slide show defining and illustrating deviant sexual behavior to professional behavioral analysis with real implications for understanding and solving cases. He changed the name of the National Academy class from *Sex Crimes* to *Interpersonal Violence* and convinced the University of Virginia to accredit it.

Roy asked me if I had yet realized the significance between being a generalist or a specialist within the Unit. He explained that in his opinion, the secret to real success and control of your work in the Unit was to develop a specialized area of expertise that was significant and notable. He suggested we team together like Douglas and Ressler had done with serial killing, but in the area of sexual crimes – an area I had taught since 1973. I pointed out that I would still not have my own specialty. He then suggested that we divide up the sexual crimes – he would specialize primarily in adult victim cases and I would specialize primarily in child victim cases. This made sense. Plus, I thought that teaching, researching, and consulting on crimes against children was important and rewarding work.

With the approval and encouragement of my Unit Chief, Roger Depue, I then began to do everything possible to improve and expand my expertise in the specific area of the sexual victimization of children. Roger Depue was an inspiring leader who encouraged his agents to pursue new and diverse interests. I read everything I could find. I attended training classes and conferences. I interacted with front line investigators and prosecutors. I studied solved cases and worked on new cases. I developed a new FBI National Academy course called *Sexual Victimization of Children*.

Recognizing that child sexual abuse was a complex and multifaceted problem, I also moved outside the circle of law enforcement and other criminal justice professionals. I increasingly interacted with and tried to learn from social workers, medical professionals, and mental health professionals. I started attending training and conferences put on by organizations such as the American Society of Adolescent Psychiatry, American Orthopsychiatric Association, University of Virginia School of Medicine, and Johns Hopkins University.

I remember hearing early on from these mental health experts that most child molesters were victims themselves, but estimates varied widely, even though they were presented as documented fact. I wondered how this could be determined, and got up the courage and confidence to ask some of these experts whom I then held in awe. I was told that the percentage had been determined by research studies in which such offenders were asked about their own victimization. I then asked how these responses were verified or corroborated. The most common answer I got was, "Why would they lie?" I was shocked that trained mental health professionals could not figure out the benefit to offenders of lying about their own victimization – the "abuse excuse." Few in law enforcement would ask such a question. These experts should have more accurately stated that most offenders *claim* to be victims. I think that good researchers would seek converging evidence from several different types of studies. Interestingly, there is some research suggesting that when sex offenders are confronted with the use of a polygraph and real consequences for their answers, the percentage claiming to be victims drops to about the same level as in the general population.

Since then, my skepticism for research concerning human behavior that is overly reliant on self-reported and self-serving information has only increased. This skepticism on my part may be due in part to a professional lifetime spent interviewing and talking with individuals who repeatedly lie about, misrepresent, and rationalize their behavior for a wide assortment of reasons. This includes most offenders and even some victims. I typically operated more from what I will call a "law enforcement bias" that tends to assume people are lying unless you know otherwise. It is more a healthy skepticism than a true bias – I do realize that some are not lying. I just don't accept something simply because someone says it. I am always attempting to assess, evaluate, and corroborate claims. As I will mention later, I have also come to prefer the terms accurate and inaccurate to truth and lie. Investigators, social workers, medical personnel, therapists who respond to child sexual abuse cases are often collectively referred to as *interveners*. The reasons people might lie or furnish inaccurate information is more diverse and complex than many interveners, including mental health professionals, realize.

As my focus on the sexual victimization of children intensified during the 1980s and early 1990s, I recognized the significance of changing and evolving attitudes about the issue. Society's prevailing attitude about child sexual abuse and exploitation could and, to some extent, still can be characterized by a kind of denial. Most people don't want to hear about it and would prefer to believe that child sexual victimization just does not occur very often and does not affect them. They certainly don't want to hear graphic details about it. Any specific discussion is quickly blunted by some version of the classic expression – too much information.

I also observed that some professionals in their zeal to overcome denial and make American society more aware of this victimization seemed to embellish the problem. Presentations and literature with poorly documented, misleading, and emotional claims were common. I thought the documented reality of the problem was bad enough. It did not seem necessary to exaggerate it. For example, I repeatedly heard that one in four females were sexually molested as children. This statistic was most often attributed to the FBI. It might be accurate, but the FBI has no data to support it. I felt that true professionals should be citing reputable and scientific studies and noting the sources of information. If they don't, when the exaggerations and distortions are discovered, their credibility and the credibility of the issue are damaged.

Exactly what was I becoming an expert in? I recognized the confusion over broad terms like *child sexual abuse, child sexual exploitation, child sexual assault,* and *missing children*. I will be repeatedly discussing in this book the importance of definitions.

Based on common usage and my analysis, I decided to use the term *sexual victimization of children* as the broadest term to encompass all the ways in which children could be sexually victimized. Under this umbrella term, I saw a wide range of sexual victimization of children: sexual abuse (intrafamilial), sexual exploitation (extrafamilial), sexual assault (peers), and sexual abduction (strangers). Not everyone defines these terms as I do. In addition, many professionals did not address or even realize the wide diversity of ways children could be sexually victimized. For many experts, a sexually victimized child was assumed to be a child abused by a parent or guardian. Their knowledge and experience with children sexually-victimized outside the family in a wide variation of ways was limited. More important, they often did not recognize how these different forms of victimization are alike and unalike and might require different intervention responses. For many laypersons, child molesters are most often thought of as weird strangers.

I came to realize that the nature of the relationship between adult sex offenders and their child victims played a significant role in the methods offenders use to access and control their victims. The relationships of sex offenders to their victims can be roughly characterized as family members, acquaintances, or strangers. Sex offenders who are strangers to their victims need only short-term access. Typically they use trickery to initially lure children, but they more often control their victims through confrontation, threats of force, physical force, and abduction. Intrafamilial sex offenders derive long-term access through their family relationships. They most often control their victims through their private access and family authority. They are providers of developmental necessities such as food, clothing, shelter, and attention. Acquaintance child molesters usually need repeated access to cultivate relationships with their victims. Of necessity, they control their victims – and such offenders may have many over a prolonged period of offending – primarily through a grooming/seduction process and by exploiting children's immaturity and developmental stages. Such techniques are the most successful approaches to gaining the victim's initial cooperation, decreasing the likelihood of victim disclosure, and increasing the likelihood of ongoing access.

In the early to mid-1980s the issue of *missing children* rose to prominence. In the emotional zeal over the problem of missing children, I recognized that isolated or anecdotal horror stories and distorted numbers were often being used. The American public was led to believe that most of the missing children had been kidnapped by *pedophiles* – a now increasingly-used mental health term for child molesters. However, children can be missing for many different reasons (*e.g.,* runaway, lost or injured, benign episode, family abduction) other than nonfamily abduction and children can be abducted by nonfamily members for a variety of reasons (*e.g.,* to solve a personal problem, ransom/profit, to kill, miscellaneous criminal activity, political) other than sexual motivation.

Many in the missing children's movement liked to say that a missing child was "any child who is not where he or she is supposed to be." It is a nice thought, but by this definition there are probably hundreds of thousands of missing children each day – every child who delays on their way to school, takes a short cut home, goes to a movie other than the one they told their parents, goes to different friend's house, plays in a secret hiding place – could be called a missing child.

The media, profiteers, and well-intentioned advocates all played big roles in this hype and hysteria over missing children. Pictures of missing children on paper bags and milk cartons and misleading claims about 50,000 stranger-abducted missing children per year were common. During my presentations and in my publications, I tried to present a more objective, balanced, and fact-based perspective based on my experience and research. I knew that most missing children were not abducted, and parents or guardians abducted most of those who were. I also knew that of those children abducted by nonfamily members, many were not missing.

By 1985, I even concluded that the term *missing children* was so vague and imprecise that it was of little value to investigators and the general public in trying to deal with the problem. There seemed to be few benefits and many disadvantages to grouping these separate areas under one label. One disadvantage was the confusion and distortion caused by calling different problems by the same name. It was like using a term like *sick children*. We are all concerned about them, but what does it mean? For medical purposes, you can't define a sick child as "any child who does not feel well." Another nice thought, but of little value in treating the problem.

During the mid-1980s, society increasingly began to deal more openly with a critical piece of the puzzle of child sexual victimization – molestation by acquaintances. These kinds of molesters have always existed, but our society has struggled to accept and understand this difficult aspect of the problem. People seemed more willing to accept a stranger or unknown father, particularly one from another socioeconomic group, as a child molester than a well-known and liked cleric, police officer, pediatrician, coach, or scout leader. The acquaintance molester, by definition, is one of us. One of the main reasons that law enforcement and the public were finally forced to confront the problem of acquaintance molestation (and organized cover-ups of the problem) was the growing number of lawsuits arising from the negligence of many youth-serving organizations – especially the Catholic Church and the Boy Scouts. And yet it still continues today – with Penn State University being a well-known example of many.

A few years back, I was asked to do a presentation at a conference of youth-serving volunteer organizations. My topic was how to identify, screen, and deal with acquaintance child molesters who sometimes volunteer to work in such organizations. When I opened the presentation up to questions, almost all the questions from the audience were about how they could protect their own children from child abductors. Nobody seemed to really want to talk about nice guys who access children through their youth-serving organizations.

And then in the late 1980s and early 1990s came what might be the ultimate form of denial of reality – the societal focus on satanic devil worshipers who were supposedly snatching, victimizing, and even sacrificing children. Many who had warned us in the early 1980s about child molesters snatching 50,000 kids a year now contended they were wrong only about who was doing the kidnapping, not about the number abducted. This seemed to be related in part to a desire for a simple and clear-cut explanation for a complex problem. This explanation has tremendous appeal because, like stranger danger, it presents a clear-cut, black-and-white struggle between good and evil (literally) as the explanation for complex issues such as child abduction, exploitation, and abuse. It was a variation of my mother's old warning about gypsies.

In the BSU, I was encouraged to put in writing and disseminate what I came to know. The diversity of the cases I studied made it clear to me that not all child molesters were the same and those differences had investigative significance. So, I developed a typology of child molesters, which was published in 1985 as a monograph titled *Child Molesters: A Behavioral Analysis*. The need was, and still is, great: Since then here have been five editions of that publication, which discusses the behavior patterns of offenders and their child victims, the National Center for Missing & Exploited Children has disseminated more than 250,000 hard copies and many more downloaded online.

In it, I explain that, although the term *pedophile* was increasingly being used, not all child molesters were pedophiles and not all pedophiles were child molesters. I also realized that those who were true pedophiles did not seem to choose their sexual preference any more than anyone else does. The 2006 movie, *Little Manhattan*, humorously but poignantly portrays the coming-of-age of a New York City boy. The boy is shown trying to come to terms with why he no longer sees a certain female classmate as a source of cooties and why he now unexpectedly wants to spend most of his time with her. I could clearly remember the summer afternoon between seventh and eighth grade when I found myself talking for hours to a girl named Terry who was about my age and lived across the street. I had known this girl most of my childhood and had never paid much attention to her. Suddenly, I was less interested in playing stickball with my friends and more interested in staring into her eyes. That summer evening, I ate my dinner as fast as I could and raced back out to see her. She became my first girlfriend. Like the main character in *Little Manhattan*, I didn't understand why this was happening to me. I later realized it's called puberty. Most notably, however, I never recall requesting to become sexually interested in a member of the opposite sex who was approximately my age. It just happened to me, as it seems to happen to most people.

Likewise, it appears that at puberty some pedophiles find themselves sexually attracted to young children. For other sex offenders, however, their sexual interest in children may be more influenced by situational factors. The important point for law enforcement and society is that, whether motivated by long-term preferences or situational dynamics, both offenders are criminally responsible for their sexual victimization of children. Psychiatry does not consider this preference for children to be a sexual orientation.

My observations and conclusions were based on the nature of my work. Although I was assigned to a Training Division, my work in the BSU increasingly involved research and case consultation as well as training. There is a simple and frequent occurrence that illustrates the interaction and value of the multifaceted kind of work I was permitted to do. I would be sitting at my desk, and the phone would ring. It was an investigator who had seen or heard of me and wanted to discuss a child victim case with me. I might spend an hour or two listening and suggesting analysis and investigative approaches. It might now be 1:00 pm and time to go teach my *Interpersonal Violence* class for the FBI National Academy. Instead of sticking to my original lesson plan, however, I would spend the time discussing my phone conversation. Because the class was made up of highly experienced and intelligent law enforcement investigators, they would provide significant feedback. I would tell them what I had suggested and they would agree, disagree, or expand on it. If the class went particularly well, I might develop the specific issues raised into a new lesson plan. That class topic would be repeated and additional cases would be submitted and accumulated. A formal research project on the topic might be implemented, and an article written and published that would spawn more case consultations.

I could not separate the training, the research, and the case consultation aspects of my work that was unfolding and transforming me into a leading investigative expert on the topic. Luckily, I never had to choose among them. It is the combining of the three perspectives that produces the highest level of expertise in any subject area. Although I sometimes had to manipulate the FBI a little, essentially they gave me the opportunity and freedom to focus simultaneously on *Crimes against Children* with what I came to call a "three-legged stool" approach: (1) developing and implementing training programs and providing instruction all over the U.S. and around the world; (2) monitoring the research of others, conducting original research, doing case studies, and writing publications; and (3) furnishing operational consultation to local, state, and federal investigators and prosecutors and testifying as an expert witness in court and before Congress. I envisioned using a three-legged stool to illustrate this inter-dependent relationship with all the legs of equal length and strength being needed to supplement and complement each other. I had a 35mm training slide made showing a stool with each of its three equal legs so labeled.

During Congressional testimony in 1983, a high-ranking FBI official was scolded during questioning about the Bureau's failure to investigate numerous missing children cases while aggressively searching for a valuable kidnapped racehorse. Ordinarily only the Director or other high-ranking FBI officials ever testified before Congress. As a result of that scolding, however, over the next three years, the FBI sent low-ranking me to testify before Congress five times about issues involving missing and exploited children. As in the old commercial for *Life* cereal, they apparently decided to "Let's get Ken" to test the waters and risk embarrassment. I did well in my testimony because I had in-depth subject matter expertise. When things later settled down, the high-ranking FBI officials again replaced me. As a result of that Congressional testimony, though, I spent a lot of time interacting with politicians and their aides and testifying many times concerning proposed legislation. I was disillusioned to learn that such hearings are usually rehearsed, scripted performances with preset conclusions based on political agendas.

The operational part of the three-legged-stool approach allowed me the opportunity to consult on and evaluate thousands of cases that I otherwise would not have had the time or the jurisdiction to personally investigate. Because most children are sexually victimized by someone they know, the earlier FBI concept of *profiling* an "unsub" rarely applied to these cases, but other types of *behavioral analysis* did. I also frequently communicated with many adult survivors and parents of alleged victims of child abuse. Most investigators are not given the time to study and research closed and solved cases. They have to move on to the next unsolved active case. In addition, when I did training, I discussed cases I worked on recently and not five or ten years ago.

The biggest flaw in how the operational type work by the FBI BSU/BAU has been portrayed in movies and television programs is their failure to recognize the difference between investigation and consultation. Many times I have been asked about the accuracy of *The Silence of the Lambs*, which won several Academy Awards. The movie was filmed in part at the FBI Academy and is rooted in the BSU's work. But as with any good fiction writer, Thomas Harris took some basic facts and then let his imagination run wild. Take the character of Hannibal Lecter. Thomas Harris asked the BSU how it expanded its knowledge of serial killers. The Unit correctly responded that they conducted research interviews of convicted serial killers and consulted with forensic psychiatrists and psychologists. Harris saved the agents some work, when he made Lector both a psychiatrist – and a convicted serial killer. Therefore, the closest basis for the Hannibal Lector character in reality is forensic psychiatrist Park Dietz, M.D. of Newport Beach, California—except obviously the serial killer part. However, at John Douglas' retirement party in 1995, I appeared dressed as Hannibal Lector to say a few words of thanks for John's inspiration.

The movie fails in accuracy, though, and in so doing fuels misunderstanding about the role of BSU agents, in its portrayal of BSU agents as conducting investigation in cases in which the FBI doesn't even have jurisdiction. If the movie were more accurate, the BSU agents would have been shown consulting on cases while on the telephone. Not only would the movie not have won any awards, most of the audience would probably have fallen asleep or walked out before it was over. Because the BSU was part of the Federal Bureau of *Investigation*, it is understandable why people would think these fictional agents investigate the cases. FBI agents in the field typically do so, but agents assigned to the BSU rarely did. They instead typically provided the less available, but valuable service of behavioral consultation and analysis in specialized areas – as I did for the last twenty years of my FBI career.

As an FBI agent I had access to detailed law enforcement and other records (e.g., investigative reports, interviews of offenders and victims, crime-scene photographs, laboratory reports, medical reports, computer records, child pornography, child erotica, collateral evidence, correspondence, recordings of control phone calls, background information, pre-sentence evaluations, prison records) that are not normally available to treating mental health professionals and academic researchers. In specific cases and if requested, forensic mental health professionals might have access to some of these records. I have strived to ensure that my observations, analysis, and conclusions concerning offender and even victim patterns of behavior are based on objective evaluation of the totality of the most detailed, reliable, and corroborated information available.

Early in my career in the BSU, I went with an experienced agent from the Unit to do a research interview of notorious, convicted serial killer John Wayne Gacy. When we arrived, there was a long list of individuals requesting interviews with him. Because we were FBI agents, we went to the top of the list, were admitted to the prison, had access to records, and were provided immediate contact with him. Again, this was a research, not investigative interview. We discussed his crimes as if we were old friends. All three of us had grown up in inner city neighborhoods – Chicago or New York. Gacy first indicated he didn't want to talk, but eight hours later, we couldn't shut him up. He was a meticulous record keeper who logged everything he did each day. He showed us how he then transferred that information to monthly summary lists of time spent on each task (e.g., eating, reading, sleeping). This was similar to the *TURK* (Time Utilization Record-Keeping) system used by the FBI to track agent work in different investigative classifications. Gacy was one of the few offenders I was aware of who had and used the interpersonal skills needed to non violently groom his child victims, but later turned to abducting and killing them. He was executed on May 10, 1994, for his heinous crimes.

Later in my BSU career, I was scheduled to go with the same agent to interview another convicted child killer. Just prior to the interview, this agent retired from the FBI. I was then teamed with another Unit member to do the interview. Because the now retired agent knew so much about the case, we requested and got permission for him to go with us. When we got to the prison, however, he was not allowed in – because he was no longer an FBI agent. These two interviews illustrate the advantages I had as an FBI agent in doing research, consulting on cases, or gathering reliable and detailed information.

Doing substantial training and research, I gradually and increasingly began to recognize the importance of definitions in my work. I realized that it was the most common terms that are in greatest need of clear definitions. When we use basic terms, we rarely define them. Apparent disagreements are often due to the confusion created by calling different things by the same name and the same thing by different names. Definitions are especially important when writing about, researching, and discussing the nature and scope of a problem. That is what I was frequently doing when conducting training, research, and in case consultation. The important point is not that terms have or should have only one definition, but that people using the terms should communicate their definitions, whatever they might be, and then consistently use those definitions. I came to appreciate this more than most investigators because of my simultaneous involvement in training and research. I therefore tried to precisely define the terms I used and then consistently use my definitions. I tried to do the same with the definitions of others.

If you spend decades doing objective training, research, and operational consultation in one specific area, you don't have to be very intelligent to develop significant knowledge and expertise. Eventually, I came to consult on thousands of cases involving deviant sexual behavior, the sexual victimization of children, missing and exploited children, and the use of computers and the Internet to facilitate the sexual exploitation of children. I became somewhat of a maverick for the first time in my life, seeing things differently than many other experts in my field. As my expertise and reputation began to grow, requests for me to conduct training and research and consult on cases also grew.

I became a founding and the first law enforcement member of the Board of Directors of the American Professional Society on the Abuse of Children (APSAC) and later a member of their Advisory Board. I was also invited and agreed to be a member of the Advisory Board of the Association for the Treatment of Sexual Abusers (ATSA). I was increasingly requested to do presentations at major national and regional conferences about the sexual victimization of children, child abuse and neglect, and missing and exploited children. During my career, I did presentations in all fifty states, Puerto Rico, Guam, American Samoa, and ten foreign countries. I was also asked and did presentations before mental health organizations such as the American Academy of Psychiatry and the Law, the American Psychological Association, and the American Academy of Child and Adolescent Psychiatry. I testified before the U.S. Attorney General's Task Force on Family Violence, President's Task Force on Victims of Crime, and U.S. Attorney General's Commission on Pornography. I also testified on seven occasions before the U.S. Senate and House of Representatives and many times as an expert witness in court.

When I was asked to testify as a key presenter at the opening hearing of the Attorney General's Commission on Pornography on June 19, 1985, I had to get special permission from FBI Headquarters. Because FBI Director Webster was going to testify the next day, there was a Bureau rule that no regular agent could speak at such a commission if the Director was presenting. Approval was obtained, but an FBI official cautioned me about the content of my presentation. It seems an FBI agent from the Laboratory Division had recently gotten into trouble for including some suggestive photos of women in his otherwise dry slide presentation on technical laboratory examinations. Someone in the audience complained. This official wanted to ensure that I wouldn't be showing any such material. I quickly explained to him that I was going to show nothing but sexually explicit material because this was a Commission on *Pornography* and that is what I was requested to do.

I was the 1990 recipient of the Jefferson Award for Research from the University of Virginia and the 2009 recipient of the Outstanding Service Award for Lifetime Achievements from the National Children's Advocacy Center. *The APSAC Handbook on Child Maltreatment* was dedicated to me: "This book is dedicated to Kenneth V. Lanning. Ken, you are one of the pioneers. You led the way. You opened our eyes. You taught us. You were always one step ahead. You're the coolest FBI agent we know. You've done more than we can count to protect kids. Thanks."

In 1995, the FBI created a new operational entity known as the Critical Incident Response Group (CIRG). The three-legged stool approach that had evolved in the BSU in the Training Division was broken up. All of the BSU's consulting and operational work and parts of its training and research work were moved into this newly-created entity. To preserve the three-legged stool nature of my work, I had a choice to make. I decided that the potential for three "legs" in CIRG was better for me than the definite two "legs" remaining in the BSU. I requested and received a transfer into what would become the BAU in CIRG. As mentioned, my actual work did not change much. I continued to specialize in the sexual victimization of children by consulting on cases but doing slightly less research and training. For example, I was no longer the instructor of record for academic classes taught to the FBI National Academy program, but I still did training presentations at conferences and seminars around the country.

Before I retired in 2000, I helped train two agents, Jennifer Eakin and Jim Clemente, transferred in to specifically help me support the FBI's new initiative on Internet child pornography named *Innocent Images*. After I retired, an entire Unit (BAU 3 – Crimes Against Children) was doing the work I had begun by myself twenty years earlier. Since my retirement from the FBI, I have continued to do training and consult on sexual victimization cases in much the same way, but with more involvement with civil litigation. For eight years after retirement, I also had a contract with the FBI under which I continued to consult with BAU 3 and testify in cases for them.

Then suddenly, on the morning of Tuesday, September 11, 2001, I was watching the morning news on television as I was preparing to leave my home. I remember being ready to walk out the door and drive to the FBI Academy to teach a class as part of this new contract when I was stood still – shocked as I watched two planes crash into the Twin Towers in the city of my birth. That was the second of two stunning historical events in my lifetime – the first being President Kennedy's assassination – during which I can clearly remember exactly where I was and what I was doing when I heard the devastating news.

The time has gone by so fast. One day I was the junior member of the BSU just trying to keep up. The next day, twenty years later, I was the senior member functioning as a bridge from past to present and helping train a whole new generation of FBI profilers and behavioral analysts. The giants who were there when I arrived had long since gone. I spent more time assigned to the Unit as a behavioral analyst than any other agent. Part of the legacy I left behind was that my emphasis on and concept of a three-legged stool to represent the equal importance of training, research, and case consultation was later incorporated into the official logos of both the BSU and the BAU. My years spent in the BSU were the best of my professional career. To paraphrase the song about *Toyland*, once I left its borders I knew I could never go back again.

I like to believe that I entered the land of the giants and left as one of them. In 1997, near the end my FBI career, I received the FBI Director's Annual Award for Special Achievement for my career accomplishments in connection with missing and exploited children.

The accompanying documentation stated:

> "Presented to Mr. Lanning for his extraordinary
> achievements in connection with missing and exploited
> children. Since 1973, he has distinguished himself as the
> FBI's point man in the study and profiling of the criminal
> aspects of deviant sexual behavior. From 1981 to 1996,
> he was assigned to the FBI Behavioral Science Unit where
> he specialized in the study of the sexual victimization of
> children. It is largely due to his hard work and research
> that the foundation of all FBI instruction and expert
> testimony in the area of child exploitation is based. Mr.
> Lanning created the curriculum in this area in which all of
> the National Academy students and newly appointed and
> In-Service FBI Agents are trained. His work is recognized
> nationally and internationally, and he is in constant demand
> as an instructor, speaker, text critic, and investigator, as well
> as a prosecutive consultant. Moreover, in 1996, he was the
> first law enforcement official to ever receive the Outstanding
> Professional Award from the American Professional Society
> on the Abuse of Children. His immeasurable contributions
> and achievements are unparalleled in this very challenging
> and critical area of investigations, and his efforts have greatly
> enhanced the public's appreciation of the Bureau's endeavors.
> Clearly, he is deserving of this award."

All of this is, of course, very gratifying, and I am deeply
thankful for the appreciation others have shown my work. But at the
same time, my specialized work also brought me some aggravation
and disappointment. My understanding allowed me to see how this
topic is often misrepresented and how its discussion is often driven
more by emotion than reality. The application of that insight is the
focus of this book. And if it happens with this issue, one I came to
know so well that I could recognize the distortions, there is no reason
to believe this doesn't happen with other issues, too.

But I'm getting ahead of myself. I need to back up to 1983.

CHAPTER FOUR

"Alright, then, I'll GO to Hell"

(Adventures of Huckleberry Finn, Chapter 30)

As I described, my first case of what came to be commonly referred to as *Satanic Ritual Abuse* began with a phone call sometime in early 1983. I tended to believe the allegations in this first case and the ones that soon followed. I had dealt with bizarre, deviant behavior for numerous years and had long since realized that almost anything is possible. Just when you think you've heard it all, along comes another strange case. The idea that a few cunning, secretive individuals in positions of power somewhere in this country could regularly commit perverted crimes and get away with them is certainly within the realm of possibility. But the number of these alleged cases kept growing and growing, until I was dealing with hundreds of victims alleging that thousands of offenders were severely abusing and even murdering tens of thousands of people as part of well-organized and intergenerational satanic cults – and there was always little to no corroborative evidence for much of it. Claims that members are born and indoctrinated into the satanic cults from generation to generation came primarily from the so-called experts on Satanism. The very reason many experts cited for believing these allegations – that many victims, who never met each other, reported the same events – was a key reason I began to question at least some aspects of these allegations. I privately sought answers, but said nothing publicly about these cases until around 1986. I knew that questioning the believability of victims of horrendous satanic ritual abuse would be very controversial. Like Huckleberry Finn in Mark Twain's novel, however, I finally decided, *"Alright, then, I'll go to hell."*

Many who have studied the allegations of satanic ritual abuse (SRA) in the U.S. believe the cases are rooted in the publication of *Michelle Remembers* by Michelle Smith and Lawrence Pazder, M.D. in

1980. This book tells the story of Smith's memories of being bizarrely victimized by Satanists when she was five years old. Her psychiatrist, Dr. Pazder, recovered these memories during therapy. Dr. Pazder was supposedly an SRA expert. In May of 1987, I was a presenter at, "The Emergence of Ritualistic Crime in America," a training seminar in Richmond, Virginia. Dr. Pazder and Michelle Smith also spoke at the seminar. Dr. Pazder said he was actually very skeptical of most SRA allegations. He claimed to know how to distinguish valid cases from false ones. I was very interested in such assessment guidance, and sat in his presentation, taking pages of notes for several hours. Together, they described the details of the rituals that *genuine* satanic cults engaged in. I began noticing something odd, though. Whenever someone asked Michelle a question about her abuse, she often turned to Dr. Pazder, who provided the answer. I finally asked them why. Dr. Pazder explained that although Michelle was the one who experienced the abuse, she didn't remember her abuse – until she went to him for therapy. He said he had captured her previously repressed memories during their therapy sessions, for months afterward. But then Michelle, he said, again lost the memories. So he became the keeper of the collective memories about her satanic abuse.

At that point, I put down my pen and stopped taking notes. During a break, they casually mentioned that they were now married to each other. This struck me as a relevant fact in evaluating the accuracy of the allegations and a possible conflict in the relationship between a therapist and patient. I later purchased a copy of their book. Maybe appropriately, I found that supposed nonfiction book on the discount fiction table at a local bookstore. I do not know who made that decision and why.

Over time, I wound up consulting on hundreds of these cases, including some from beyond America's borders. Due to my national FBI position and reputation, I became a kind of informal clearinghouse for specific cases, as well as the phenomenon in general. As more and more of cases – which contained very serious allegations – came to my attention, I became progressively more concerned about the lack of physical evidence and corroboration. I was extremely troubled by the lack of corroborative evidence when there should have been such evidence, especially with claims of multiple offenders, blood ritual, torture, and murder.

Eventually, I began to mention this skepticism to investigators who contacted me. Whatever my own suspicions, though, I still knew the allegations needed to be objectively investigated. Such serious claims needed an objective investigation. I was never a strong proponent of SRA, but I decided to hold my tongue. I wasn't going to speak out publicly about my concerns until I conducted more analysis and research. I didn't feel like it was appropriate for me to openly question the allegations of so many victims – without a defensible basis for those doubts.

I recognized that those cases all involved allegations of what sounded like child sexual victimization – but with a combination of certain atypical dynamics. I began defining the cases by the following four significant dynamics they seemed to share:

1. Multiple victims (who were very young when the abuse began),
2. Multiple offenders (often alleged to be part of an organized group),
3. Fear as the primary controlling tactic, and
4. Bizarre or ritualistic activity.

Those allegations primarily came from groups of young children or from older adult survivors whose memories of victimization began in early childhood. They described being subjected to strange games, insertion of foreign objects, torture and mutilation, killing of animals, photographing of satanic activities, and wearing of costumes. Interestingly, the young children's accounts didn't seem quite as bizarre as those of the adult survivors and contained fewer memories of murder and human sacrifice.

The cases all involved unsubstantiated allegations of victimization, which made them difficult to either prove or disprove. Yet, it increasingly seemed like many of the unsubstantiated allegations simply had not happened. Those cases generally called into question the credibility of victims of child sexual abuse and exploitation. They also added to controversies over complex topics such as the suggestibility of children, the reality or reliability of recovered repressed memory, and diagnoses such as *Multiple Personality Disorder* (MPD).

Debates were sparked over how the human brain stores and recovers memories – and how easily children can be led and influenced by those asking the questions. Those cases were the most polarizing, frustrating, and baffling of my career. And I've encountered some extremely bizarre and unusual cases during my more than forty-plus years of studying the criminal aspects of deviant sexual behavior.

I was not alone with my concerns. By 1985, problems related to investigating and prosecuting several high profile cases – one in Jordan, Minnesota and another at the McMartin Preschool in California – became nationally and publicly known. I was well aware of both of these cases. In February 1985, I coordinated at the FBI Academy what I believe was the first national seminar held to specifically examine such cases. This seminar was *not* designed to teach anybody anything. Instead, it brought together criminal justice professionals, currently responding to such cases, to better define them and evaluate what we knew – or didn't know – about them. As time went on, SRA cases were also discussed at many regional and national conferences that focused on the sexual victimization of children and MPD; an increasingly questioned psychiatric diagnosis now called *Dissociative Identity Disorder* (DID).

Difficult questions were being raised. Some of the victims' allegations were physically impossible – including claims of victims being cut up and put back together and offenders taking a building apart and then rebuilding it. Certain allegations were possible but improbable – including claims of human sacrifice, cannibalism, vampirism, and organized groups active over many generations. Many allegations were possible and probable – including use of child pornography and victims being cleverly manipulated by offenders. Other allegations were corroborated – including medical evidence of vaginal or anal trauma and offender confessions.

I was left scratching my head and wondered: How could there be so much fear and concern over so many children being victimized by a large intergenerational satanic conspiracy with so little hard evidence? I was forced to consider that what alleged victims, professional interveners, and mental health experts claimed happened simply had not. And if those allegations didn't happen, I increasingly asked myself these four key and pertinent questions:

1. "Why are the victims alleging it?"
2. "Where are they getting the details?"
3. "Why is there a similarity to the victims' stories?"
4. "Why do so many intelligent, well-educated professionals believe it?"

I identified and considered many possible answers. The first is apparent: *clever offenders.* The allegations may not seem to be true or accurate, but they are. The criminal justice and child welfare systems lack the knowledge, skill, and motivation to get to the bottom of this crime conspiracy. The offenders were born and indoctrinated into their satanic cults for generations. Investigators don't know how to investigate these cases. Perpetrators have infiltrated the government and law enforcement.

Confronted with a lack of evidence, some conspiracy advocates expanded the scope of the alleged conspiracy. It wasn't just one FBI agent involved in a cover-up. No, instead it was the entire FBI, then the entire Department of Justice, and then the *Zionist Occupied Government* (ZOG) that controls the country. ZOG is an abbreviation referring to an anti-Semitic conspiracy theory alleging that "Jewish agents" have secretly taken over the U.S. government.

A few people even claimed the CIA was the true perpetrator behind the satanic allegations. They were conducting mind control experiments. They believed the allegations about satanic cults constitute misinformation deliberately planted by the CIA to discredit any victims who came forward. Some advocates, who believed all these allegations were valid, told me those offenders were so clever they deliberately pretended to be dumb or disorganized to fool society and the police.

In short, they said the fact there was no proof – was proof!

Any objective professional responder or intervener evaluating victims' allegations of ritual abuse cannot ignore or routinely dismiss the lack of physical evidence, the difficulty in successfully committing a large-scale conspiracy crime, or human nature. Many people don't understand how difficult it is to commit a crime that involves numerous co-conspirators.

One clever and cunning individual has a good chance of getting away with a well-planned interpersonal crime. Bring one partner into the mix and the odds of getting away with it drop considerably. The more people involved in the crime, the harder it is to get away with it. Why? Human nature.

People become angry and jealous. They begin to resent the fact that another conspirator is getting a larger share. Once caught, they decide to make a deal for themselves by informing on their partners. If and when members of a destructive cult commit murders, they're bound to make mistakes and leave evidence behind. Eventually, they even brag about their crimes or make a deal to reduce the charges against them. In a lifetime of studying human behavior, I've never met humans who don't make mistakes. Ask anyone who has planned a complex social event – they know that if something can go wrong, it will go wrong.

Even if only portions of the allegations are inaccurate, what then are the answers to the questions I was asking? From a law enforcement perspective, I focused on finding evidence. That was vital to determine if crimes had occurred. For my own satisfaction and curiosity, if nothing else, I wanted answers. After consulting for many years with psychiatrists, psychologists, religious scholars, anthropologists, folklorists, therapists, social workers, child sexual abuse experts, prosecutors, and other law enforcement investigators, I could find no single, simple answer. Instead, a complex set of dynamics seemed at play. And, depending on the case, those dynamics could be different.

To briefly summarize here, possible answers to my questions include:

1) Pathological distortions linked to processing reality when influenced by underlying mental disorders such as dissociative disorders, borderline or histrionic personality disorders, or psychosis;

2) Traumatic memory with fear and severe trauma causing victims to store their memories in fragments that can distort reality and confuse events;

3) Normal childhood fears and fantasy rooted in a shared cultural mythology of ghosts, monsters, and boogeymen under the bed;

4) Misperception, confusion, and trickery involving clever offenders deliberately introducing elements of the occult, simple magic, drugs, and other techniques to deceive children who have little frame of reference for sexual activity;

5) Overzealous interveners causing something referred to as "intervener contagion," by asking repetitive questions, leading or suggestive questions, rewarding and bribing victims for providing more or specific details, or making assumptions about or misinterpreting what the victims actually said;

6) Urban legends that spread realistic stories concerning recent or alleged events with an ironic or supernatural twist.

One of the great urban legends during my law enforcement career pertained to something called "snuff films." I first heard about them in 1973. More recently, they were allegedly available on the so-called *dark web* portion of the Internet. They're the Holy Grail of pornography – long sought after, but never found. I used my FBI experience to evaluate their existence. First, the term *snuff film* must be precisely defined. I didn't invent this definition. It comes from the legend. *Snuff films* are described as visual depictions (but not limited to film); of individuals (humans, not animals, who were alive at the beginning); who are murdered for production value (the script called for it, not an accident or death caught on video); for the sexual gratification of viewers (a type of sexual pornography, the worst of the worst); and the image is disseminated for commercial profit (allegedly for huge sums of money, and not just kept for the producer's personal gratification).

During my career, I have encountered several cases where sexual killers produced a visual record of the torture and death of their victims. This was done for their personal collection and gratification. But those are not snuff films because they don't fit the definition in the legend. Although snuff films could exist, I have never found one. Not one that could be documented by objective medical, technical, and behavioral analysis. In my opinion, this isn't because people are incapable of such horrible behavior. They clearly are.

But it's extremely risky to disseminate a visual record of a murder you committed. Using technology and with far less risk, images can easily be simulated to look like *snuff films*. We have all seen movies whereby every criterion known to the average person it appears someone was murdered. So, *simulated snuff films* have been around for a long time.

Skeptics of SRA allegations also wanted answers. Some people who doubted the allegations simplistically blamed the whole phenomenon on overzealous therapists (i.e., iatrogenic/physician induced) or on those who interviewed the children. That was insufficient and doesn't explain many of the cases I knew about. An alleged victim's account can also be influenced or contaminated by misperception and confusion, other victim's accounts, and suggestions and leading questions from parents. Most so-called ritual abuse cases probably involve some combination thereof. They could also include other, as yet unknown to me, explanations.

Knowing more about Satanism seemed to be a key to better understanding those cases. While I didn't just arbitrarily decide to become an expert, I did read everything I could find, communicated with scholars, and attended a variety of training conferences on the topic of *Satanism*. During my research, I even came across people who believed the Pope was the anti-Christ and Roman Catholicism was witchcraft. And along the way, my expertise about the sexual victimization of children inadvertently led me to become the FBI expert about Satanism, the occult, and cults.

Ultimately, I found that most people define Satanism essentially as any religious belief system other than their own. My personal Catholic education was based on religious values and supernatural explanations. From an objective law enforcement perspective, however, it makes no difference what spiritual belief system is used to enhance and facilitate or rationalize and justify criminal behavior. Only the law, not the Ten Commandments, matters in criminal investigations.

But the intent and motivation for any alleged ritual activity is potentially very important. Prosecution could be jeopardized if acts can be defended as constitutionally protected religious expression. In the presentation I heard in Richmond, Virginia, in 1987, Dr. Pazder said the ritualized abuse of children involves "a systematic use of symbols and secret ceremonies designed to turn a child against itself, family, society, and God," and "the sexual assault has ritualistic meaning and is not for sexual gratification."

Many ritualistic acts, satanic or not, are simply not crimes. I was raised in a religion full of rituals. Almost all religious parents indoctrinate their children into their own belief system. Mutilating a baby's genitals for sadistic sexual pleasure is clearly a crime. On the other hand, male circumcision for religious reasons is most likely not. What about female circumcision, whether for religious or cultural reasons? Does it constitute child abuse? In addition, if someone alleges that certain criminal acts were committed under the influence of, or in order to conjure up supernatural spirits or forces, this could form the basis for an insanity or diminished capacity legal defense.

After three years of consultation, research, networking, and analysis of those cases, I finally felt confident enough about my analysis. I decided I could publically express my skepticism, the basis for it, and my recommendations for an objective investigative response. I realized there was a reasonable, but unpopular middle ground – a continuum of possible activity. Some of what the victims allege may be true and accurate, some may be misperceived or distorted, some may be symbolic, and some may be contaminated or false. The problem, however, is determining which is which. The job of a professional investigator is to listen to all victims, assess and evaluate the relevant information, and conduct an appropriate investigation to find out what happened and consider all possibilities. I realized I had no choice but to openly and professionally share the results of my research.

I decided to disseminate to criminal justice professionals and then others what I had learned about those cases from a law enforcement perspective. Whenever possible and appropriate, I included it in training programs I conducted and presented, such as the classes for law enforcement officers attending the FBI National Academy. I spoke about it at law enforcement in-service training, professional seminars and meetings, and regional and national conferences on child abuse and sexual victimization. I even gave presentations about this subject at the 1991 American Psychological Association Annual Conference in San Francisco and the 1994 American Academy of Child and Adolescent Psychiatry Annual Meeting in New York City.

Recognizing the limited audience for presentations, I also disseminated my findings in written and published format. In 1992 the U.S. Department of Justice and the FBI published my monograph entitled *Investigator's Guide to Allegations of "Ritual" Abuse*. It was distributed at no cost by the FBI and also has been posted by numerous groups on the Internet, where it can still be downloaded from some of these sites. People have asked why I have allowed certain groups to post it on the Internet. In short, I have no control over that. I was a federal employee, working on government time, so my publications could not be copyrighted. I can only hope those who post and disseminate it, do so in its entirety.

Because I wrote it while I worked for the FBI, the publication has frequently and incorrectly been referred to as the "Lanning Report" or an "FBI Investigative Report." While it does contain the results of my research and case consultations, it is a training monograph on the topic. Although approved by my FBI superiors, peer reviewed, and published by the Department of Justice, it does not represent an official FBI position on Satanism. Neither was it a guide for parents, nor one for therapists or clerics. As the title indicates, it was intended to be a guide for *investigators* to better understand the nature and scope of these cases – as well as the best practices for investigating them.

In the monograph, I discuss recommended law enforcement responses to SRA and other so-called "satanic crimes." I point out that signs, symbols, and rituals can mean anything that practitioners want them to mean and/or anything that observers interpret them to mean. The meaning of symbols can also change over time, place, and circumstance. For instance, is a swastika, spray-painted on a wall, an ancient symbol of prosperity and good fortune, a recent symbol of Nazism and anti-Semitism, or a current symbol of hate, paranoia and defiance? Is it intended to recruit, frighten, or to get attention? I discussed this perspective in a presentation I once did for a group of prosecutors. One of the prosecutors, identifying himself as Jewish, interrupted and objected. He said that everyone knows the swastika means one thing and one thing only – anti-Semitism.

Considering the Holocaust, his response was understandable – but still inaccurate. To get notoriety, some rebellious individuals will do whatever will most shock and outrage society. Spray-painting a circle or meaningless numbers achieves the same property damage – but not the same societal response. I believe quiet and rapid cleanup might produce better results than roping off the area and calling eyewitness news. Few people seem to agree with me and instead overreact emotionally. This gives the perpetrators exactly what they want and increase the likelihood of more incidents and imitators. Occasionally, individuals claiming to be victims perpetrate such incidents themselves to get attention and sympathy. These are good reasons not to jump to conclusions.

Few people understand one type of false allegation or claim. It's related to what mental health professionals call *Factitious Disorder,* or *Munchausen Syndrome.* With this psychological disorder, an individual seeks secondary gain, such as attention or forgiveness, by falsely claiming to have done something *(e.g.,* heroic rescue, awards, furnishing information to solve a crime) or have had something happen to them *(e.g.,* illness, vandalism, hate crime, assault, rape). *Factitious Disorder by Proxy* or *Munchausen Syndrome by Proxy* is a close cousin, in which an individual seeks the same secondary gain, but through something done by or to another individual associated with them such as a child, parent/guardian, or friend. This syndrome can be caused or influenced by an assortment of psychological conditions and disorders, but by definition the individual making the claim knows it is inaccurate or a lie.

In the criminal justice setting, these disorders are often manifested as false or fabricated crime victimization. Even experienced investigators are often baffled by factitious disorder cases because they cannot imagine why an individual would lie about these events. Investigators usually look for more traditional motives such as money, anger, jealousy, and revenge. But the key to identifying these disorders is to understand that people sometimes lie to get attention and forgiveness. Then investigators will be alert for such motives and needs. These are the unpopular but documented realities that must be considered when evaluating allegations and claims.

It would have been easy for me to sit back, as many people did, and say nothing publicly. But I spoke out and published because I was concerned about the credibility of child sexual abuse victims. I was outraged that guilty people might get away with molesting children because children's credibility was called into question in all cases. I was of course also concerned that innocent people might be falsely accused.

And I was outraged that in cases involving these fantastic elements, real abuse was being hidden and identification of sexual abuse perpetrators was blocked. All because we couldn't also prove they were satanic devil worshipers who engaged in brainwashing, cannibalism, and human sacrifice! Or that they were part of a large conspiracy spanning generations.

Unlike when I spoke up about how the issue of missing children was being distorted, I didn't anticipate the negative reaction of some of my professional child abuse and law enforcement colleagues. When I finally went public with my concerns and doubts about these cases, some claimed I had gone to the "dark side." A few even accused me of being a Satanist who had infiltrated the FBI to facilitate a cover-up. Both Sister Evelyn, my 6th grade teacher at St. Nicholas of Tolentine Catholic grammar school (who was sure I was going to be a priest), and my parents would have been shocked to learn that.

Yet, how does anyone disprove such allegations? Or should they even have to? I invite anyone hearing such allegations to carefully consider the source and the evidence. And although reluctant to dignify such absurd accusations with a reply, I can only say to anyone who made such allegations, "You are wrong."

Others, however, claimed I was part of a witch hunt and helped create the hysteria that led to these bizarre and false allegations. As proof, they pointed to "Child Pornography and Sex Rings" a January 1984 article I co-authored for a special issue of the *FBI Law Enforcement Bulletin* (*LEB*) on pedophilia.

As mentioned, in 1990, I received the University of Virginia Jefferson Award for Research for my research on ritualistic abuse of children. Later, objective surveys and studies on these types of cases by the Michigan State Police, Virginia Crime Commission, Utah Attorney General's Office, a Department of Health and Human Services funded university research project, and a commission in Great Britain have all confirmed the essence of my analysis and findings.

What did all this mean beyond the narrow issue of SRA? I eventually came to realize that the last of my four questions was actually the most significant: Why do so many intelligent, well-educated professionals believe something is happening when it isn't? This included some in the media and well-respected celebrities. Over time, the reality of these types of cases had become obvious to me. They were essentially implausible. So why did I see it when so many other professionals didn't? Was there something wrong with them – or me? Why was there such a strong negative reaction to my logical presentations of my analysis and experience? Why did people come up to me at the end of my presentations and claim I said things I didn't or that I did not say things I did? Why did dedicated believers of satanic ritual abuse of children repeatedly thank me for writing a publication that actually expressed skepticism about these cases? How could so many people believe things for which there was little or no evidence? Why would normally skeptical law enforcement officers accept material produced by religious organizations, photocopies and images of newspaper articles, and video recordings of television programs as evidence of, or law enforcement intelligence about, the existence and nature of a significant crime problem?

These questions plagued me – until I gradually recognized an important and basic characteristic of all adults. This includes child sexual abuse professionals. For me, the answer to this last question is so significant I will repeat it over and over: regardless of intelligence or education and often despite common sense and evidence to the contrary, *adults tend to believe what they want or need to believe; the greater the need, the greater the tendency.* The extremely sensitive and emotional nature of child sexual abuse, and the fact that the concept of Satanism carries some measure of religious significance, make this reality an even bigger potential problem.

Along the way, I also recognized that anyone emotionally involved in an issue is often one of the least reliable sources of accurate information. If you want an objective evaluation, people who are reasonably objective must do it. For example, parents might be appropriate sources of information about what it feels like to have one's child sexually victimized or abducted. They are not, however, appropriate or reliable sources about the nature of the larger problem – or what the police did or should do in an investigation.

However, those emotionally involved individuals are the very people who often receive the most attention by the media, politicians, and society. For a current example, just look at the media and political response to the healthcare debate, the killing of young children at their schools, and gun violence in general. Personal and political perspectives tend to dominate emotional issues like these, as well as child sexual abuse.

In the early 1990s, in the midst of media interest in satanic ritual abuse, producers for CNN's *Larry King Show* contacted me. They were doing a show about SRA and wanted to interview me. I asked who else would be on the program. When they said that one of the guests would be an adult survivor of such ritual abuse, I politely declined. I have repeatedly turned down media requests to participate in a debate with alleged victims, or with emotional zealots. It may make for good ratings, but it does little to help inform and educate people and puts professionals like me in a difficult position. I believe it's improper to blur and confuse the distinction between these different perspectives.

Several hours later, the producers called back with a counterproposal. The adult survivor would come on first and tell her story. There would then be a commercial break, and she would leave. The program would continue with two mental health professionals and me talking about SRA. I thought that compromise would at least keep the emotional and professional perspectives separate, and I agreed to participate.

While the program was airing, I sat in the green room listening to the alleged adult survivor of satanic ritual abuse. She described her participation in the cult and in the mutilation and murder of over a hundred children. Her participation would have made her the most prolific serial killer in U.S. history. So if she was credible, I wondered why no one detained her and called the police to arrest her. They gave her airtime, but apparently did not think it was their job to take any action. She then moved off the set and the program continued with the professionals.

I tried as best I could in that limited format to convey the findings of my research and consultations on these types of cases. When the phone lines opened up, however, many callers seemed to not understand the essence of what I had said. They even asked me how to identify such satanic cults in their community. I began wondering if the media are effective at communicating a professional perspective on important and complex issues. I was trying to get people to look at these cases reasonably and objectively. Yet I often reluctantly agreed to media interviews on various topics primarily to bring some joy to the life of my elderly widowed mother who enjoyed seeing her son on television. Most of today's media seem to have little interest in calm, balanced, rational discussion. Maybe that's because the public has little interest in it.

Several years later, my former BSU partner, Roy Hazelwood, asked if I was ever on the *Larry King Show*. I told him I was and what the topic was.

"You must be the one," Roy said.

By then Roy had retired, but, like many retired FBI agents from the BSU, he was doing consulting work. He and the group with which he worked were consulting with Chris Carter, the creator and producer of *The X-Files*.

They had asked Carter where he got the idea for the program. Carter explained that while watching an edition of the *Larry King Show*, an FBI Agent had explained how he could find no real evidence corroborating many bizarre alleged satanic crimes. So Carter began wondering if such unusual cases led some people to be so skeptical that a specialized unit was needed to investigate them.

Thus, *The X-Files* was born. I laughed to myself. How ironic that my efforts to get laypeople and interveners to look more objectively at these cases apparently played a role in creating a science fiction television program about FBI agents investigating nonsense like visits by extraterrestrial life. The program seemed to add to mistrust of the government and wild conspiracy theories. In fact, tourists visiting FBI Headquarters in Washington, DC would sometimes ask the tour guide where the X-Files unit was. One media critic even opined that there was no better place to get a dose of conspiracy paranoia and nutty sci-fi. Although the program may have been successful and entertaining for many viewers, its perspective was fictional and to some degree resulted in the exact opposite of what I was trying to convey.

One *X-Files* episode airing on January 27, 1995, did, however, express my perspective almost verbatim. The character named Scully points out that the FBI conducted a seven-year study of occult conspiracies, but found little or no evidence of alleged murders. Scully's dialogue was taken, almost word for word, from one of my publications. And an April 2015 episode of *Criminal Minds*, a program almost as unrealistic as *The X-Files* – paid my work homage, when the fictional FBI BAU characters mention the "Lanning Report," twice! They were discussing a case involving alleged victims of SRA and a debunked therapist who interviewed them back in 1985 when the victims were four years old. Since I never watch these programs, I learned of this episode when my sister in New York called me after watching it and hearing her maiden name.

I was contacted on SRA-type cases on a fairly regular basis until around the mid-1990s when such inquiries gradually slowed to a trickle. The growing backlash of skeptics seemed to quell the tide of the reports. To this day, however, I am still occasionally contacted concerning allegations that seem to fit many of the dynamics of these ritual abuse cases, albeit somewhat different. For example, with more recent cases, there is less emphasis on Satanism and more on other conspiracy-related groups. Some of the material I wrote about this topic continues to be available on the Internet, so people still occasionally communicate with me about such cases.

I spent more than forty years addressing the issue of sexual victimization of children. Only a very small part of that work involved Satanism or cults. Oddly enough, though, if you Google me, there are far more references concerning my work involving SRA and Satanism than anything else. Whenever I have been contacted about such cases, I usually start by making the same two general recommendations: 1) minimize the satanic/occult aspect and, 2) keep religious beliefs separate from the investigation.

I have consulted on hundreds of cases in which large numbers of individuals – victims and interveners, investigators and prosecutors, mental health professionals and the media – believed something happened that did not. My experiences with these kinds of cases and what I learned profoundly changed first my professional and then my personal life. It eventually became the inspiration for this book.

CHAPTER FIVE

"The Witch Hunt and the Backlash"

As the debate over *Satanic Ritual Abuse* of children moved into the 1990s, more and more people began to recognize that the repeated failure of investigations to find the kind of corroborative evidence that should have existed was significant. In time, the media changed its focus and generally began to express an increasingly skeptical view. For example, *Frontline* aired several TV programs for PBS where they analyzed and raised doubts about several major cases, and the phenomena in general. Professionals were becoming increasingly polarized over the issue. In my national role at the BSU, I regularly interacted with the media, individuals, and organizations discussing all aspects of this issue. Slowly, I began to identify certain common characteristics and behavior patterns exhibited by the protagonists in this debate. The two extreme points of view started to be referred to by observers as *"the witch hunt and the backlash."*

I realize that the sexual victimization of children is a highly charged, intensely emotional issue. I saw how publicity and controversy over complex topics such as satanic ritual abuse, repressed memory, and the suggestibility of children divided and polarized many child advocates, the media, and the American public. And in controversial and highly publicized cases, persons at one extreme often claimed that interviewers easily manipulate children and the allegations are frequently part of a big witch hunt led by overzealous fanatics or incompetent and money-hungry experts. Those at the other extreme repeatedly claimed that victims do not lie about sexual abuse, every act happened exactly as alleged, and the skeptics alleging otherwise are part of a powerful backlash led by child abusers or those denying the extent and reality of child sexual abuse. Varying media coverage, movies, articles, and opinions about high-profile satanic ritual abuse cases such as the McMartin Preschool case in Manhattan

Beach, California, which played out between 1983 and 1990, exemplified this highly polarized controversy.

There is a big problem in discussing this polarization. It is the terms often used to label the extremes. I reluctantly use the terms they used for each other: the *witch hunt* and the *backlash*. But keep in mind—these terms are subjective, judgmental, derogatory, and poorly defined. To address this, and to be consistent with what I had come to believe, I tried to define the terms as I use them here and when I wrote a 1996 article about my observations that I titled, *The "Witch Hunt," the "Backlash," and Professionalism*. By describing their characteristics, each extreme is presented almost as a caricature of itself.

The *witch hunt* is characterized by the tendency to exaggerate child sexual abuse, to believe the children, and to criticize the criminal justice system – for a perceived failure to properly investigate or when an accused abuser is acquitted. When child sexual abuse is alleged, they assume it happened, and then do everything they can to try to prove it.

The *backlash* is characterized by the tendency to minimize child sexual abuse, to emphasize false allegations, and to criticize the criminal justice system – for aggressive investigation or for obtaining convictions of innocent subjects. When child sexual abuse is alleged, they assume it has not happened and then do everything they can to try and disprove it.

Of course, because these definitions are vague, not all the traits attributed to either the witch hunt or the backlash can be found in everyone who might be considered a member – of either group.

In spite of their polar-opposite views, the witch hunt and the backlash are very much alike. They are essentially two sides of the same coin. I began identifying some of the characteristics that both sides seemed to share. What then struck me as even more important is that these shared characteristics are not unique to the so-called witch hunt and backlash. They are, in fact, common characteristics of zealotry, extremism, and confrontation.

For instance, substitute any of today's opposing, polarizing viewpoints – left wing/right wing; Fascist/Marxist; conservative/liberal; pro-life/pro-choice; traditional/progressive – and you'll see many of the same characteristics. We see them every day in emotional and political discussions. See if any of these common, shared characteristics seem familiar to what you see, hear, or read on any given day, whether online, in blogs, in newspapers, on talk shows, network and local news, CNN, MSNBC or Fox News.

1) Cross Labeling. Each side develops negative labels for, and defines the nature and characteristics of the other. Neither side, however, uses these negative labels to identify itself. No one in the witch hunt, for example, believes that he or she is taking part in a witch hunt, just as no one in the backlash believes that he or she is involved in a backlash. In fact, each side vehemently denies it. Both sides are quick to use derogatory labels (such as racist, homophobe, misogynist, Nazi, Fascist, hater, alt-left, or antifa) to refer to the other – but resent it when these terms are applied to them. Most important, each side takes great delight in talking about, making fun of, and criticizing the other.

2) Polarization. Each extreme tends to take an all-or-nothing approach to complex issues. You are either with them or against them. Forget the middle ground. Dialogue with the other side is seen as consorting with the enemy – and constitutes guilt by association and betrayal.

While in the FBI, a woman claiming to be an adult survivor of satanic ritual abuse called me. She insisted a satanic cult was trying to kill her. I told her to contact the police immediately. She said she'd been working with an occult crime task force in her city that included the police. But, she claimed, the satanic cult had recently murdered her sister and only members of this task force knew where her sister had been hiding. This caused her to realize this task force was actually made up of Satanists masquerading as anti-Satanists. That's when I asked why she was calling me. She explained that the occult crime task force had always told her the one person she should never contact about her victimization was me. That's how she now knew that I was the only person she could trust. If I was not against her, I must now be with her. I was familiar with the task force she referred to and her account about them telling her not to contact me was likely. But based on my experience, I had strong reservations about the accuracy of the rest of her account. Because there was nothing I could personally do to protect her, I encouraged her to contact the state police with any evidence she had.

Each side disseminates written material about their cause or beliefs and brings together individuals of like beliefs. When someone from the "other side" is invited to participate, it's primarily as a token gesture. The extremists then can ridicule his or her "absurd" views. In the name of political correctness, when someone with opposing views speaks, you interrupt and shout them down.

Thinking about these dynamics, can't you picture much of the current political commentary on television or online? Both extremes attack anyone who seems to take a position in the middle. Today it's seemingly unpopular to hold moderate views on many subjects. But moderation is not necessarily a bad thing. I actually felt proud when I was accused of being part of both the witch hunt (a zealot spreading exaggerated stories of child sex rings) and the backlash (a Satanist infiltrating the FBI to prevent the uncovering of Satanic Ritual Abuse). So, I took comfort in a quote I found attributed to Abraham Lincoln, "If both factions, or neither, shall abuse you, you will probably be right. Beware of being assailed by one, and praised by the other."

3) Attack the Messenger. Each side focuses its attacks and criticism on the person of the messenger – rather than on the substance of the message itself. This is known as an *ad hominem* attack. It is easy to claim (and difficult for the accused to disprove) that the witch hunt is composed of fanatics with personal agendas, antifamily views, and one world government plans or that the backlash is composed of radicals, pedophiles, and Satanists attempting to conceal their activity. One way to personally attack and dismiss the messenger is to simply label him or her as part of the *witch hunt* or *backlash* or some other negative or narrow-minded group. Hitler and the Nazis were evil and murdered millions of people. Stalin and the Communists were evil and murdered millions. Yet, people today frequently compare disliked individuals or groups to Hitler and the Nazis, but rarely to Stalin and the Communists. In many circles, expressing anti-Fascism views is considered free speech to be supported; expressing anti-Marxism views is considered hate speech to be attacked. In 2017, Papa John's Pizza issued a statement that it is "open to ideas from all. Except neo-Nazis." Communists acceptable?

4) Appeal to Emotion. Each side relies heavily on raw emotion. As a result, they frequently hold forth anecdotal examples of victims, adult survivors, innocent children, or falsely accused parents, describing their personal tragedies in graphic detail. The media in particular usually gravitate towards an emotional – rather than objective – discussion of issues they cover. Emotional backstories grab ratings during coverage of sports, talent competitions, and the daily news.

In my opinion, you can have an emotional or a professional discussion about important issues, but not both at the same time. Sometimes, today's journalism makes it is hard to tell which is happening. The same thing could be said for professional conferences. I was on a panel at one such event, debating allegations of satanic ritual abuse with a professional therapist. Imagine my surprise when he suddenly announced that he was a victim himself and he knew what it was like not to be believed – a totally emotional argument. I lose the debate.

I was once on the Anderson Cooper cable news program debating the value of a law requiring sex offenders to have green-colored license plates on their cars. Also on the program with me was the state senator who had proposed the legislation. Terms like *child predator* and *violent sex offender* were quickly being thrown around with no clear definitions. This is a problem. We have long warned our children about accepting rides from strangers. Based on this legislation, were we now supposed to tell our children to only avoid accepting rides from strangers with green license plates? When I asked exactly how this law would protect children, the state senator didn't answer. Instead, he told the story of a young girl murdered by a convicted sex offender who approached her while driving a car.

Then he added the new law would be named after her – an emotional approach having nothing to do with the effectiveness of the law. And again I lose the debate.

In any public debate between emotion and reason, emotion almost always wins. This is one reason why naming these laws after victims is such an effective strategy for getting them passed whether or not they are likely to be effective.

An emotional appeal often involves the use of specific terminology. For example, the **same** case of sexual victimization could be referred to as, 1) a teacher had a physical relationship with a teenage student, 2) a pedophile molested a child, or 3) a predator raped a baby. Depending on which terms you use to describe the victimization, you will trigger different emotional responses.

The words chosen have impact. I once heard a TV commentator claim that it was wrong to use the term *illegal alien* because aliens are from outer space. What's the difference between a *new religious movement* and a *cult*? Between a *camp* and a *compound*, between *conversion* and *brainwashing*, or between *education* and *mind control*? How about between *martyrdom* and *suicide*? What's the difference between an *illegal alien* and an *undocumented immigrant*? Often it isn't what happened or a precise technical distinction – but simply the emotional point being put forth as part of an agenda. That's what we need to carefully consider before coming to conclusions or taking action.

I hear varying verbs used to describe the Russian involvement in the 2016 presidential election, and as this book goes to press, it continues to be investigated. Did the Russians try to *influence* or *meddle* in the election? What precisely do those terms mean? Are they the same as to *rig, fix,* or *alter*, as in intentionally changing the actual results? If so, is this a new form of election sabotage? Based on my experience, the former Soviet Union or Russia has been "meddling" in U.S. politics since at least 1970. Their primary goal has been more to fuel divisive conflict and disorder and less to elect a specific candidate. Former FBI Deputy Director Andrew McCabe seems to agree. At a 2017 Cyber Summit, CNN.com quotes him as having said, "The fact is, the Russians have been targeting us with everything they have over the last 50 years."

5) Distortion of Facts. Each side conveniently fails to define its terminology, or inconsistently uses the terms it does define. When we want volume to support our viewpoint, a "child" is defined as anyone younger than eighteen. When we want impact or mention specific examples, a "child" soon becomes anyone under the age of twelve. Both sides frequently cite information out of context, and selectively quote only that portion of an article or research that supports their view. In spite of their well-known inaccuracies – unnamed sources, newspaper articles, Internet blogs, and television commentary or news magazine programs are often used as primary sources of information. And today's distortions are quickly and widely disseminated to eager believers by e-mail, chat, text message, Facebook, Twitter, Snapchat, and other on-line social media services.

Zealots often generalize, going from a few cases to all cases. They make the unusual and atypical seem common and typical. Megan's Law, Jessica's Law, and the Adam Walsh Act are the best-known laws that determine how the criminal justice system deals with all convicted sex offenders. But these laws were named for child victims who were abducted and murdered.

The plain truth is this: Most child molesters **do not** abduct their victims and most offenders who do abduct their victims **do not** kill them. Statistics bear this out. So then, should these laws, passed in response to atypical sex offenders, be applied to all sex offenders?

6) Conspiracy Theories. Both sides seem to need to believe that the other side – often perceived as their enemy – is part of a national, international, or well-disciplined organization with a carefully orchestrated and implemented master plan and strategy. They see *proof* of this conspiracy every time three or more people with similar views, actually or allegedly, meet or contact each other. They believe, or claim to believe, that their side simply *meets*, *trains*, and disseminates *factual information*. At the same time, they argue that the other side *conspires*, *brainwashes*, and disseminates *propaganda*.

For some people, this conspiracy concept includes the notion that the other side has especially targeted them for persecution. They find it difficult to understand that each side, and every group in between, suffers from the same disorganization, diversity, dissension, and disagreements.

Any complex human endeavor will always contain unexplainable or chance factors and unavoidable mistakes. Even in the extensively planned and successful killing of Osama Bin Laden, the Navy SEALs who executed that mission had to leave behind the tail of the classified helicopter that crash-landed in Pakistan. But conspiracy theorists will ask for explanation of this or that, taking advantage of the fact that most people don't have the time or expertise to research and refute their claims.

But someone does know the explanation or answer.

Take one of the highly emotional allegations involving Bill and Hillary Clinton. One of my former BSU colleagues was assigned by the FBI to be part of the Vince Foster investigation. A former Clinton appointee, Foster was instrumental in hiring Hillary at the Little Rock, Arkansas, law firm where he worked. He later left his post there to become deputy White House counsel during Bill Clinton's first term as president. Foster later committed suicide.

As a result of my colleague's extensive knowledge about Foster's death, learned through a lengthy objective investigation, he is one of the few who can logically and factually respond to every reasonable issue raised by those who claim Foster's death was a conspiracy-driven homicide.

Of course, such logical and factual arguments rarely change the opinion of zealots. I've seen this firsthand, due to my own extensive knowledge and experience about sexual victimization of children. So it's easier for me to recognize how zealots misuse and distort information that surrounds this emotionally charged topic.

Proving the negative is impossible. So it's difficult to disprove conspiracy theories. Only after I was accused of being part of such a conspiracy – one that I knew did not exist – could I prove the accusers wrong.

But, I could prove it only to myself.

Satan's Silence: Ritual Abuse and the Making of a Modern American Witch Hunt, a 1995 book about ritual abuse, tries to explain the roots of this "plague." Under the heading "Receptive Officials" on p. 113, the authors say, "Congress, for instance, directed the FBI to focus on solving cases involving missing, murdered, or sexually exploited children. The agency sponsored a conference on the subject in May, attended by law enforcement officers from around the country, and devoted an entire issue of its *Law Enforcement Bulletin* a few months later to sexual abuse and sex rings."

That all sounds very ominous, organized, coordinated, and conspiratorial. It also implies a connection between the congressional directive and the FBI conference and publication.

I have no personal knowledge about such a directive from Congress to FBI Headquarters and no one ever communicated it to me. No one ever directed me to get involved in this area of sexual victimization of children. As I have described in detail, I did so totally on my own for mostly self-serving reasons. Because I was a relatively low-level FBI agent at the time, I struggled for years to get the FBI more aggressively involved in fulfilling its investigative responsibilities in federal child sex abuse cases. Eventually, the FBI did.

However, I do know a great deal about the May 1983 conference and the January 1994 special issue of the FBI publication, the *Law Enforcement Bulletin* (*LEB*), the book mentions. Both were **totally** my idea. Neither one had anything to do with any efforts by Congress — or any other part of the government. Nor did they have anything to do with ritual child abuse cases.

I had talked my Unit Chief into sponsoring the 1983 conference on sexual exploitation of children so I could expand my expertise into the subject matter I was then specializing in. At the time I planned that conference, I had never even heard of ritual child abuse. My intention was to specifically learn more about sexual exploitation of children and network with the few law enforcement experts who then worked in this field. I identified and invited them by name. That conference was more of a think tank – with attendees as presenters. No one in Congress played a role, or even approved the conference or its agenda. As a side note, when the National Center for Missing & Exploited Child was being formed at the time, its organizers were trying to contact law enforcement experts on this topic. They discovered that the few such experts they were seeking were not available at their offices. I had also identified them and almost all of them were then attending that 1983 conference at Quantico.

What about the special issue of the *LEB* mentioned in the book? It came about because I had a pile of submitted articles on my desk. I had been assigned to do peer reviews, because they were all related to child abuse. One day it just popped into my head to put several of them together in a special-themed issue on child sexual abuse. The editors at the *LEB* agreed and it was done. To the best of my knowledge, that was the first issue of the *LEB* in which all the articles had a common theme. It was also the first one to be reprinted.

There is absolutely nothing in that issue of the *LEB* discussing ritual child abuse. One article co-authored by me does discuss child sex rings. Such sex rings were clearly defined and continue to constitute a real and well-documented type of case, which is poorly understood even today. That same article is also significant because I believe it is the first to describe how a child molester used a computer in committing his sex offenses.

No conspiracy or organized master plan by the government was involved in either the conference or the special issue of the *LEB*. They were just some spontaneous ideas I came up with by myself to do my job more effectively. I can't say if those two events unintentionally influenced anyone's attitudes causing him or her to believe allegations about ritual child abuse. The fact is, that I, more than any one person, after becoming aware of these extreme allegations, played a major role in discrediting them – after I took the time to carefully study and analyze them.

As mentioned, some people even claimed I was part of a satanic conspiracy, sent to infiltrate the FBI and facilitate a cover-up of these cases. I know the truth – but can't prove it to anyone other than myself. No amount of proof will change the mind of most believers.

They believe conspiracy theories, not because of any real and objective evidence, but because they want or need to. They selectively accept and reject facts based on their personal agenda or bias.

7) Claim to Special Knowledge. Those on each side claim they somehow know *with absolute certainty* the facts of any case or situation. They know things that the investigation, prosecution, courts, and scientists cannot determine with any amount of certainty.

They know exactly what the Russians did in the 2016 election, long before the investigation will be completed. They infallibly know who is guilty and who is innocent, and who is right and who is wrong. They are certain of these things, in spite of the fact that most of what they know came from biased opinions (theirs and other's), unnamed sources, gossip, rumors, myths, bloggers, social media, or media accounts. Inaccurate and biased accounts are then repeated and circulated to justify their conclusions and convince others.

And then there are those who even claim that what they know comes from God. The legend becomes fact. But without the criminal justice system or some other neutral arbitrator, there is no consistent independent standard about who did what.

8) Selective Use of the Criminal Justice System. Although there are guilty people who have not been convicted and convicted people who are innocent, the often-repeated standard in the U.S. is that "people are innocent until proven guilty." Conversely, this seems to imply that people proven guilty should be considered guilty. Yet, some debating an issue want to selectively use these standards in making their arguments. In fact, I have even been criticized for using criminal convictions in my research. The assumption, I guess, is that I should have instead used one group or the other's opinions.

This has become a big problem in our society. Each side decides for itself when an investigation, conviction, or acquittal has meaning and which court orders should be obeyed. They use and cite criminal justice decisions only when they suit their purposes. They quote court findings of guilt as proof of their position only if someone *they* believe is guilty is convicted. If someone *they* believe is innocent is convicted, then the court decision is irrelevant, ignored, or attacked. If the conviction is overturned on appeal, the court decision and the system are then praised and cited.

They want *justice*, but define it as the conviction of those they believe are guilty. They, and not the courts, decide. There's one problem. However imperfect, it is the criminal justice system – not emotionally involved zealots – that decides who is guilty. In that system, *not guilty* is different from being *innocent*.

A case in point occurred as I watched a recent cable news program. The female moderator and an expert were discussing declining female births in relationship to male births in India, due to selective abortion. They discussed the cultural and financial reasons for this. The expert mentioned that abortions based only on the gender of the fetus were now illegal, but the laws were not really being enforced. The host seemed surprised. "The law is the law," she emphatically said.

Here's my question: Would the host have responded the same way if they had been discussing something like undocumented immigrants being deported, homes being foreclosed, or a President issuing an executive order that superseded a law she disliked? I don't know, but quite often the concept of "the law is the law" only seems to apply when we agree with the specific law in question.

I've attended child abuse conferences where alleged adult survivors of satanic ritual abuse were introduced as victims, but then talked about the role they played, carrying out unspeakable violent crimes against children. Yet most in the audience still embraced and forgave them. Their violent behavior, the alleged adult survivors said, was part of their victimization. But if you can get attention and forgiveness for mutilating and killing children, for what other lesser failures in your life will you be held accountable? Being a victim may explain some behavior – but it does not excuse all behavior.

9) Manipulation of and by the Media. Both sides aggressively try to influence and use the media. They cooperate with any level of the media – if they believe their views will be aired and supported. But in their zeal to manipulate the media, they forget that the media often manipulate them. Depending on which way the wind is blowing, today's media often fluctuate between witch hunt and backlash-type stories. Ratings drive stories. Which position is more popular or appealing can change. Today, some in the multifaceted media increasingly seem to have almost permanently taken sides. Instead of being objective fact-finders they are supposed to be, they encourage, or are part of, extreme views on many issues.

When covering such issues, much of the media also seem to gravitate toward divisive and polarizing, rather than informative responses. I was once on a CNN news program to discuss Amber Alerts, which are sometimes issued for missing children. When I arrived at the studio, I couldn't understand why another expert and I had intentionally been placed in separate interview rooms. As I listened in my provided earpiece to the on-air questioning of the other expert, I discovered the reason.

"For an opposing view, we now go to Ken Lanning," the host said. There was only one problem: I agreed with almost everything the other expert had just said. So why did that network portray us as dissenting and extreme opposites – instead of as professionals with some differing positions or views that could be calmly and reasonably discussed? My guess is controversy for ratings!

10) **Self-deception**. Sad to say, neither side can see its own mistakes. They don't believe they do any of the above, while asserting the other side does all or most of them. They accuse the other of doing these things, but are outraged when someone accuses them of the same.

"We" are objective and right. "They" are devious and wrong.

Currently people protest violence, hate, and lack of inclusion – by engaging in violence, hate, and exclusion.

I once watched a television program about unexplained cattle mutilations. One group of guests explained how the mutilations were the work of satanic cults. The other guests explained how the same mutilations were obviously the work of aliens from outer space. During the program, each group attacked the other's arguments as absurd and ridiculous, and not based on objective evaluation. Which group was correct? Neither. Later, more objective research determined that most of those cattle "mutilations" resulted from the natural process of bloating, blowflies, and buzzards and not Satanists or aliens!

Whether an unfair, distorted personal attack by the media is supported and repeated or condemned and protested is usually determined solely by who is being attacked. Without realizing it, both sides believe, hear, and see what they want to believe, hear, and see. This is by far the most important and universal characteristic of zealotry and extremism. For example, today the long-established news networks such as ABC, CBS, NBC, and cable news network MSNBC and CNN are quick to attack the distortions and bias of the FOX News network. But those same networks seem incapable of recognizing – and will vehemently deny – that, they often do the same things and vice versa. Commentators ridicule the statements of politicians they dislike by making statements that are inaccurate and often just as ridiculous.

After I recognized those characteristics, I felt that the best approach was not to imitate them. Instead, I chose to respond with professionalism. Behaving with professionalism is not the same as simply claiming to be a professional. Some individuals in professional positions are also zealots and extremists. In addition, people who clearly are not professionals might also consider following these guidelines.

I think most would agree with me that the following characteristics are consistent with integrity, objectivity, and professionalism, as well as conducive to objective fact-finding.

1) Deal primarily with issues, not personalities. Those behaving professionally understand that individuals who disagree with them are not necessarily bad or evil – they recognize the merit in dissenting views, and minimize the focus on individuals while maximizing the discussion of issues. That's why I deliberately try to limit naming of names and excessive use of specific, detailed case examples here. The messenger's agenda may be a factor in their opinions or conclusions, but professionalism understands that there are extremists on both sides. Advocating this doesn't suggest that people's credentials, character, and motives should never matter.

2) Evaluate hidden agendas. We can examine complex problems such as the sexual victimization of children from three major perspectives that I call the "3Ps." They are the personal, political, and professional. The *personal* perspective encompasses the emotional: how the issues affect our individual needs and wants. The *political* perspective encompasses the practical: how the issues affect our getting elected, obtaining funding or pay, and attaining status and power. The *professional* perspective encompasses the rational and objective: how the issues affect people and what is in their best interest. Often these perspectives overlap or are applied in combination. Because most of us use all three, sometimes the perspective in control may not be clear. The media and others often blur these three perspectives.

Some professional interveners who respond to child sexual victimization cases often seem to have personal wants and needs that may affect their ability to objectively evaluate allegations. These can include such things as wanting or needing to believe that: all child victims are typically innocent, offenders are typically evil, sexual activity between adults and children is always unwanted by the child, their work is special, and the problems keep getting worse.

Personal and political perspectives tend to dominate the response to emotion-laden topics like child sexual abuse, religion, immigration, sexism, and racism. These personal and political perspectives are reality and will never go away. In fact, they can and have achieved many positive things. I came to believe, however, that complex issues such as sexually victimized children, the budget deficit, climate change, healthcare, gun violence, and the economy, need more people to address them from the professional perspective and fewer from the personal and political perspectives.

Carefully consider and evaluate agendas driven by personal and political perspectives. Parents and victims have every right to express how they feel about their victimization. That doesn't mean, however, that their emotional opinions should be **the** primary basis for determining the nature of a problem, for telling law enforcement how to investigate cases, or legislatures what laws to pass. It seems clear that in our society emotional and anecdotal stories of individual victimization carry a lot of weight in determining attitudes and allocating resources.

3) Strive for objectivity. Objectivity is critical for law enforcement professionals. It's also important for anyone engaged in fact-finding, where his or her conclusions are important and where accuracy is crucial. To increase professionalism, people need to keep an open mind and try to control their emotions. Idealizing children, common even at professional child abuse conferences, fuels emotionalism.

In my former FBI office a brass plaque with the FBI seal on it reads, "Herein Toil the Ever Vigilant Guardian Angels of America's Children." While poignant, I believe those kinds of appealing but emotional sentiments can interfere with objective fact-finding. An FBI agent involved in investigating online child sexual exploitation cases was quoted by name in a newspaper article as saying, "I don't mean to be facetious, but it's like doing God's work, I'm excited as heck to be here."

You can debate the advantages and disadvantages of an investigator truly believing this. But the advantages or disadvantages of publically stating the sentiment are another matter. It may come back to haunt you during later testimony in a case. In my religion, all work is viewed as God's work – I agree.

Those professionally dealing with child abuse are not guardian angels doing some special version of God's work; they are dedicated, hardworking individuals trying to do an important job. This also raises the complex and difficult question of whether individuals or professionals with strong political or personal agendas can even be objective. While many can rise above their direct or indirect victimization and their individual or practical needs, some delude themselves by claiming they can or have done so.

4) Consider the middle ground. Most complex issues have room for differences of opinion. Sometime during my Catholic education, I remember a teacher quoting in Latin from Horace, "In medio stat virtus." This means virtue stands in the middle or virtue is in the moderate – not the extreme – position. Some nights I would flip back and forth between MSNBC and FOX and wondered how media reports about the same story could be so different. My experience tells me that the accurate version is usually somewhere between the two extremes expressed.

Most people would agree that just because one detail in a story is accurate doesn't mean that every detail is. But many people seem to believe that if you can disprove one part of an allegation or story, then the entire allegation or story is false. To either totally believe or totally disbelieve everything is always easier than acknowledging the complexity of a situation. But few complex events or situations have one simple cause or explanation.

5) Critique yourself first. This may be the most difficult responsibility of true professionalism. It is easier to point out the mistakes of others, especially when admitting your own might expose you to ridicule or a lawsuit. I knew a police officer who was very active in spreading and publicizing claims of satanic ritual abuse. He eventually realized he had allowed his personal religious beliefs to overwhelm his law enforcement objectivity. He acknowledged that there was no real evidence and he had made mistakes in judgment. Most important, he tried to undo some of the damage his training may have caused by publicly admitting his mistakes. This is an extraordinary individual, one we should admire. It would have been far easier for him to say nothing and just fade away.

Those responding professionally should spend more time thinking about what they are doing and less time worrying about what the extremists are doing. The bad behavior of others does not justify your own bad behavior. We need to make sure our own houses are in order and our information is accurate and reliable before criticizing others.

While working as an expert witness, I learned that one of the most damaging things an expert can do to his own credibility is to fail to admit the merits of obviously correct statements, and points of view of the opposing side. Holding on to indefensible positions makes you look foolish and stubborn. One way to defuse extremist attacks is to occasionally admit that some mistakes were made. One effective way to counteract the influence of extremist behavior is to not attack or imitate them, but to do one's job in a competent, objective, professional manner.

6) Strive to improve knowledge and skills. Those striving for professionalism recognize the need to grow, add to their existing knowledge, and sharpen their skills. To do this, they read a variety of books and articles, including those presenting alternative or different views. They attend seminars and conferences with minds open to a diversity of thoughts and ideas. They engage in honest dialogue with responsible individuals with differing views. That's because listening only to opinions with which they already agree makes true growth difficult. They also try to stay current on the latest research in their respective fields. Anyone trying to form opinions and make important decisions will benefit from these valuable lessons.

7) Evaluate and use information properly. Those being professional and others making important decisions don't overly rely on newspaper articles, online blogs, and television programs as the primary source of information and basis for their opinions. Anyone who has ever been involved in a publicized case or has significant expertise knows that many of the details reported by the diverse media are inaccurate. Yet, we usually assume the details of other reported cases or situations are accurate, especially if those details happen to agree with our opinions and beliefs. So professionals should verify original sources of information and properly reference research.

In the early days of FBI research, members of the BSU interviewed incarcerated serial killers. We used a protocol, but we were new to such research. We asked them about their interest in a wide range of areas. One of these areas was pornography. The problem, though, was that we didn't precisely define the term or determine the killers' exact involvement with pornography. In essence, the research found that about 81 percent of serial killers reported some interest in what they believed to be pornography. If anything, this percentage is probably low and consistent with most men. Individuals, however, repeatedly use this vague finding as proof of pornography's role in murders by serial killers.

In fact, a quote on one anti-pornography website says, "I was aware of an FBI study of thirty-six serial killers conducted in the 1980s, which revealed that twenty-nine of these killers were attracted to pornography and incorporated it into their criminal sexual activity, including serial rape-murder." Whatever the role of pornography in sex crimes is, this FBI study should not be misrepresented or misused to make the point.

In another example, noted researcher David Finkelhor and his co-workers wrote an article about what their research indicated about the true nature of the problem of online sexual exploitation of children. When the print media learned about the article, they ran it under the headline, "Fears of Internet Predators Unfounded, Study Says." The story told of a new study by the Crimes against Children Research Center, at the University of New Hampshire. At that point, I was flooded with phone calls and e-mails from law enforcement colleagues who read or heard about the headline or newspaper story in print or online. They wanted to know who the crazy, academic fools at the University of New Hampshire were. That's because from their investigative work, they knew the problem of online predators was large and serious.

I told them that it would be a mistake to abandon their investigative efforts just because an academic research study determined the problem was not significant. Just as it would be if they dismissed the study, ridiculing it as the work of naïve academics. The proper professional response before taking any action, I said, would be to obtain and read the *entire* published study – not just a media article about it.

When they did, they would discover the full article does not state that online sexual victimization of children is **not** a problem. Instead, the study says the nature of this problem is different from common stereotypes. My conclusion? It's usually a big mistake to rely primarily on limited portions, or only the media, when making decisions with significant consequences.

Another example involves citing undocumented emotional claims that fit an agenda. I have repeatedly heard that "Child pornography (or prostitution) is getting much worse. The child victims are getting younger and the sex is getting more violent/perverted." I cannot say for certain that's inaccurate, but I have my doubts. I believe there's always been a broad spectrum of such victimization. My greatest skepticism, though, comes from the fact that I first heard this claim in 1978. That was almost forty years ago!

Professionals should clearly define their terms and then consistently use those definitions, unless indicating otherwise. Operational definitions for cited terms such as *child*, *sexual abuse*, and *ritual abuse*, used in research should be clearly communicated, reconciled, and not mixed together to distort findings.

I concluded that the so-called backlash had both a positive and negative impact on the investigation and prosecution of sexual victimization of children cases. In a positive way, it reminded criminal justice interveners of the need to do their jobs in a more professional, objective, and fact-finding manner. In a negative way, it cast a shadow over the validity and reality of child sexual abuse, and has influenced some interveners to avoid properly pursuing cases.

Much of the damage caused by the so-called backlash, however, was actually self-inflicted by the so-called witch hunt and some well-intentioned child advocates. The mistakes of some overzealous interveners and the insistence by a few of the literal accuracy of unfounded bizarre allegations of satanic ritual abuse fueled the backlash, letting it influence public opinion. To this day, when questioning the validity and reliability of children's allegations, defense attorneys will still point to cases like the McMartin Preschool case in which hundreds of children alleged things that were never corroborated or proven.

On the other hand, the debate over the validity of such grotesque allegations has obscured the well-documented fact that children can be reliable witnesses and that there are child sex rings, bizarre sexual preferences, and cruel sexual sadists.

In his 2014 book, *The Witch-Hunt Narrative*, Ross E. Cheit sets forth his research indicating that there are seeds of truth in allegations in many of the controversial daycare cases. I tend to agree with many of his findings. I was in the middle of the issues and cases described and discussed in Cheit's book. I consulted on and have first-hand knowledge of most of the cases he discusses, including the McMartin Preschool, Kelly Michaels, and Frank Fuster cases. I have previously communicated with many of the investigators and prosecutors in the cases examined in the book.

However, I found an issue with the book. As I wrote in a 2017 commentary in the *Journal of Interpersonal Violence*: "Cheit believes that there were unjustified charges against the majority of the accused in the McMartin case but then chooses to focus on the evidence of 'some abuse' by one of the accused and not on the reasons for all the unjustified charges. That choice of focus makes the book interesting but less meaningful for investigators." Cheit does not really explain how a fairly typical daycare case turns into an atypical nightmare convincing to so many trained professionals. I have been searching for such answers for a long time.

Advocating professionalism doesn't mean that we cannot have or express strongly held beliefs and opinions. However, we must carefully consider and evaluate the basis for those beliefs and opinions and understand how they affect our decisions.

Old Lanning Family Vacation at Parks'
Boarding House in Freehold, NY 1950

On a Date in Central
Park with Kathy and her
Younger Siblings 1966

Wanting to Get Married, Navy OCS Graduation
Ball, Newport, RI 1967

EOD Qualification Wearing Deep-Sea Diving Suit, Navy Base, Newport, RI 1967

Commissioned March 10, 1967

*Navy EOD and Underwater
Swimmers School Patches 1967*

*2nd from Left at Morning Formation, Underwater Swimmers School, Key West, FL
1967*

Kathy and I on Our Wedding Day,
Tolentine Church, June 1967

San Antonio Division SWAT Training, FBI Academy Quantico, VA 1973

Hazardous Device School, Redstone Arsenal, AL January 1974

Cover of the January 1984 LEB Special Issue on Pedophilia and Cover of the So-Called "Lanning Report" on SRA 1992

Teaching FBI National Academy Class, FBI Academy 1992

My 1993 Red Miata - A Selfish Man's Car?

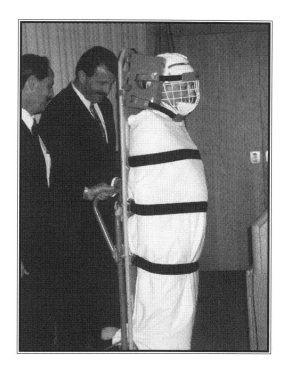

Me Impersonating
Hannibal Lecter during
John Douglas' Retirement
Party 1995

Receiving Director's Annual Award for Special Achievement 1997

In Front of St Basil's Cathedral during Training in Moscow, Russia 1998

*My Three-Legged-Stool Concept later
Incorporated into BSU/BAU Logos*

Cover of Monograph "Child Molesters: A Behavioral Analysis" - 5th and Final Edition 2010

New Lanning Family: Brian, Me, Kathy, Rick, Christi, Mike, Max, Kyle, and Melissa

"You're not Saying Now What you Did Five Years Ago"

One day over lunch, Roy, my BSU partner of many years, and I were talking in the FBI Academy *Boardroom*, where the faculty usually ate. We agreed that after about seven years of extensively studying the criminal aspects of deviant sexual behavior, we both felt like we knew everything there was to know, which made us experts. But we both continued researching and learning for many more years. And somewhere along the way, we began to change from thinking we knew everything to wondering if we knew anything.

With each new day and case, I tried to test my hypotheses, beliefs, and opinions. After I made a training presentation in the early 1990s, an investigator who had attended one of my previous presentations came up to me and said, *"You're not saying now what you did five years ago."* I considered this a compliment for two reasons. First, when studying human behavior you **should** change. Every day is a learning opportunity, a chance to gain new insights. Second, someone recognized that I had, in fact, modified my attitude and approach.

Consulting on large numbers of cases involving allegations of satanic ritual abuse changed my mindset and approach to other types of cases, too. My experience with ritual abuse allegations reminded me of what I was first taught in FBI New Agent training back in 1970. I was supposed to be a neutral, objective fact-finder who goes in with an open mind and lets the investigation take me wherever the evidence leads. When reviewing submitted case materials, I increasingly questioned the source and reliability of any information set forth. During BSU case consultations, I became a nuisance by persistently and repeatedly asking, "How do you know this; how do you know that?" – As investigators and prosecutors were presenting the summary of their cases. How I evaluated information had changed forever.

I was assigned to the BSU, analyzing behavior for twenty years and could have retired as early as 1994. With my almost four years of military service, accumulated sick leave, and twenty-five years with the FBI, I could have collected most of my salary without even going to work. At the end of my career I was essentially working for less than minimum wage. I chose to stay six more years primarily because I enjoyed what I was doing. I had the greatest job in American law enforcement. I handled almost all the cases coming into the Unit involving non-fatal sexual victimization of children by family members or acquaintances and many of the child abduction cases. I was consulting on many high-profile cases, there was little paper work, and my supervisors left me alone. I was helping to stop individuals from victimizing children. It was a rewarding, fulfilling, and enjoyable job.

I included my new insights, definitions, and concepts in my research, lesson plans, training presentations, and in material I developed for publication. I updated my monographs published by the NCMEC with additional editions. One of the monographs included two Appendices consisting of protocols to organize the investigation of multivictim, multioffender cases such as SRA. From 1995 to 2018, I wrote or coauthored numerous book chapters and articles (*see* Appendix III).

Concerning research, I wound up managing the "Serial Child Molester and Abductor Research Project" and the "Abductors Who Murder and Kidnappers of Newborn Infants Program." Both were funded in part by the U.S. Department of Justice and involved research interviews of convicted offenders and case studies. The results were published by the NCMEC.

The Kidnappers of Newborn Infants research project was a variation in my work. It involved child abductions committed almost exclusively by women and not motivated by more common reasons such as sexual gratification, profit, ransom, revenge, and/or power.

The cases apparently were motivated by the need to have a child to fill a perceived void in the offender's life. Because there were only about a dozen such cases each year, the research included almost every known case and not just the typical sampling of cases. The focus of this research project was defined by two criteria: the age of the victim and the motivation for abduction. The cases studied involved the abduction of children six months of age or younger for nontraditional motives. The age criterion was fairly straightforward, obvious, and the reason for the common descriptive term "infant abduction." The motivation criterion was more complicated, uncertain, and the reason for the less used term "nontraditional abduction."

Prior to this research, it was commonly believed those women kidnapped babies either to replace an infant they had lost or to experience a vicarious birthing of an infant they were unable to conceive or carry to term. Although there were cases fitting those dynamics, the research surprisingly found that the most common motivation was the belief that presenting their husband, boyfriend, or companion with a newborn allegedly fathered by him might hopefully maintain or save the relationship. That is why they didn't adopt *a baby*, but instead faked a pregnancy resulting in *his baby*. Society and the media still seem to prefer to repeatedly portray the abductors as sad and unfortunate women who just wanted a replacement baby to love.

The old forty-hour road school trainings I did for law enforcement were gradually replaced by shorter presentations for multi-disciplinary audiences. Thanks to the vision of Lt. Bill Walsh and the Dallas Police Department, a class that I first taught with Brian Killacky of the Chicago Police Department in 1987 attended by about forty police officers evolved into an annual Crimes Against Children Conference attended each year by over 4,000 investigators and other professionals. I have presented at it many times over the years.

What follows isn't a detailed discussion about the *sexual victimization of children*. But I wanted to briefly mention a few key concepts concerning the subject, which I came to understand over my long career. These are insights that are not commonly perceived by society nor typically communicated by the media and many child advocates. They're ideas that I came to recognize as I applied my newly energized and critical thinking skills. To illustrate them, I include some personal stories and examples.

Much of what I discuss here is set forth in more detail and context in my various publications, especially the 5th edition (2010) of my monograph titled *Child Molesters: A Behavioral Analysis for Professionals Investigating the Sexual Exploitation of Children* (*see* Appendix III).

Diversity of Cases
Different types of cases require different intervention protocols.

One of the first things I became more sensitized to was the significance of the diversity of cases. The sexual victimization of children involves varied and diverse dynamics. It can range from one-on-one inside the family abuse to multioffender/multivictim outside the family sex rings; from stranger abduction of toddlers to prostitution of teenagers; and from the collection of child pornography to its production and distribution.

What might work in one type of case might not work (or could even cause problems) in another. Be careful about making generalized statements and implying they pertain to all cases.

Importance of Definitions
Disagreement is often just confusion over definitions.

I became sensitized to the importance of awareness about definitions and their consistent use. That's because I continually saw the problems that resulted from a failure to do so. At times, however, I did wonder if my concern over definitions was a valid concern or excessive analysis. But I saw how definitions played a critical role in understanding and misunderstanding, making them very important. It's especially confusing when the definitions of common words are arbitrarily changed to make a point. And it happens all the time. People and groups even pressure the publishers of dictionaries and the media to use the definitions they prefer. You cannot hope to determine the nature and scope of a problem, or find solutions, if those involved cannot precisely define it. Doing research requires clear and consistent operational definitions. Comparing research then requires reconciling differences in the operational definitions used.

In polarizing debates and heated discussions, few people pause to clearly and consistently define their terminology. I learned that arguments over things such as the pervasiveness of child pornography, number of missing children, and registration of sex offenders were not always a matter of a difference of opinion. What appear to be disagreements and differences of opinion ("alternative facts") is often the result of confusion over definitions.

Even the choice between the terms *molestation* and *rape* when referring to the sexual victimization of children is significant. In 1985 I was invited to present at a large anti-pornography conference being held at a major American university. Many of the attendees were either conservative Christians or liberal feminists. These distinct groups tended to agree on few social issues other than their strong opposition to pornography, but for different reasons and with different definitions of what it is. Pornography was and still is a complex and controversial issue. The focus of my presentation, however, was limited to child pornography. Early on in my presentation, I pointed out that my topic was less contentious because, unlike with adults, children cannot consent to be in pornography. Plus the resulting visual images are always illegal.

During a break, several women approached me. The first one was quick to tell me that she disagreed with my comments concerning consent by adult women. She said that women are brainwashed and cannot truly make such decisions, due to our male-dominated society. I actually enjoy discussing such dissenting opinions. As we engaged in an intense but respectful discussion concerning this, however, the second woman standing nearby was becoming increasingly agitated. She finally interrupted and told the first woman to leave me alone and stop harassing me. She proclaimed she knew I was right because when she was twelve, she had been sexually "molested." With that, the first woman replied that she knew I was wrong because when she was twelve, she had been "raped."

Thus began a heated disagreement. With that, I politely walked away. Ever since then I have wondered, why, although both women were apparently sexually victimized at the age of twelve, one identified herself as a child who had been *molested* and the other as a female who had been *raped*.

Recognizing that not all cases are the same, I suspected this was most likely influenced by the details and dynamics of their individual victimizations. Over the years, I have thought about this incident many times and speculated about what those circumstances specifically were.

When using more common or everyday terms, we rarely define them. However, many such common terms have a wide range of possible definitions – all correct but often different. Each person thinks he or she knows the definition, and so doesn't question it. I call them fill-in-the blank terms. When people hear or read the term, they usually insert their own definition. These include terms commonly used such as *crazy, missing, violence, justice, abuse, rape, pornography, predator, stranger, friend, murder, bullying, sex,* and *child*. Some users subtly change or expand the definitions of such terms when it suits their purpose. For example, *violence* may include emotional violence, *abuse* may be any corporal punishment they disapprove of, *pornography* may be any sexually explicit material they don't like to view, and *missing* may mean a five-year-old abducted by a sex offender or a sixteen-year-old running away.

Child Abduction
There is not an epidemic of child abductions by sex offenders.

Nonfamily child abductions, often imprecisely referred to by laypeople as stranger abductions or *stranger danger*, are not always sexually motivated. When I joined the FBI in 1970 and someone spoke about the abduction or kidnapping of a child, it was immediately assumed the case was a ransom-motivated abduction by a criminal. Within my law enforcement career, less than twenty years later, that initial assumption (or strong suspicion) drastically changed. By then, it was assumed the case was a sexually motivated abduction by a sexual predator. Obviously neither assumption is always correct. In fact, each is unlikely to be true without further information.

The traditional FBI perspective of profit motivation had been rooted in a law passed in response to the Lindbergh ransom kidnapping in 1932. That famous case did involve a ransom. But the FBI simply did not look for *missing* children. It did investigate federal *kidnappings*. The established assumption was that in the absence of reliable witnesses, a kidnapping was determined primarily by receipt of a ransom demand. Today, the FBI uses a wide diversity of criteria to evaluate whether a missing child may have been abducted and then aggressively responds with its many resources.

Sexually motivated nonfamily abduction is probably the one aspect of sexual victimization of children that people think occurs more than it actually does. People tend to underestimate the likelihood that a family member or trusted acquaintance will sexually victimize their child, but overestimate the likelihood a stranger will. The prevailing perception today is that little children are highly likely to be abducted by sexual predators. Although it is hard to know for certain, I am aware of no research that indicates that children today are any more likely to be abducted by sexual predators than they were forty or sixty years ago. But with the twenty-four-hour national news cycle, the media certainly reports more frequently on any individual cases.

I learned from BSU research that the primary, but not the only, reason some child molesters used violence and abduction to control their victims was they lacked the interpersonal skills to do otherwise. These types of research findings were disseminated through BSU training programs and published material.

John Wayne Gacy in Illinois and Gary Arthur Bishop in Utah were two well-known exceptions to this research finding. Each man had good interpersonal skills and had groomed and seduced many boy victims who had been acquaintances. At some point, their sadistic needs and urges increasingly drove them. This led them to also abduct and murder victims who were essentially strangers. Because of this, both men escaped identification for a time. Each of them was eventually identified and stopped when they made the mistake of abducting and murdering children to whom they could be linked. Gacy and Bishop were each convicted and executed.

Predators?

Although popular, use of the term can be counter-productive.

For a variety of reasons, the term *predator* appears to have increasingly become the preferred term to label any adult who sexually victimizes a child. When referring to such sex offenders, it's become the term of choice for the public, media, politicians, child advocates, and law enforcement. The popularity of the NBC *Dateline's* "To Catch a Predator" added to this trend. Using the term predator makes things simple. It primarily appeals to, and serves the purposes of, the personal and political perspectives. Just using the word seems to provide some level of emotional gratification. State and federal statutes even include the term in their titles. But the word does little for the professional perspective.

To illustrate the conflict, during the late 1990s, I was invited to take part in a multidisciplinary group discussion in Washington, DC. The meeting's focus was finding ways to improve the criminal justice response to sexually victimized children. The issue of definitions and the best terminology arose. I expressed my concern about the increasing use of the term predator, when referring to offenders.

"For me," I said, "it's almost a step back to the dirty old man stereotype."

This seemed to quickly enrage some of the participants. They wanted to contact the Director of the FBI and demand I be disciplined or fired. I couldn't understand this extreme reaction. The purpose of the meeting was to exchange ideas. Those I offended could have simply and calmly disagreed with me and explained why.

Not long after, I suspected the reason for their disproportionate response. Some of the attendees had been Congressional staff members. They knew that Congress's proposed 1998 federal crime bill (which later became law) was named the Protection of Children From Sexual **Predators** Act (emphasis added).

The term *predator* has no precise or clear definition. More significant for laypeople, the term has a very negative connotation and conjures up an image of evil in disguise and inevitable violence. Many offenders do exhibit behavior that is predatory in nature. But in my experience, the most prolific, persistent, and predatory child molesters rarely use violence to manipulate and control their victims. They typically use a *grooming* process. They engage in predatory sexual behavior but are *not* violent sexual predators. In addition, by any common definition, some child molesters do not engage in predatory sexual behavior. They might victimize one, available child.

I believe the term *predator* especially should not be used in prevention programs. Doing so makes it more difficult for both adults and children to identify potential molesters. Staff members, parents, guardians, and program participants who are on the lookout for evil predators will be less likely to recognize the nice guy molester who is pleasant, kind, and helpful, as the most successful acquaintance offenders usually are. Unfortunately, but understandably, this problem persists. Recent victims of a sports doctor accused of molesting hundreds of girls and young women over many years while he worked for USA Gymnastics referred to him as "monster." As will be mentioned below, nice guys who nonviolently groom their victims can be child molesters.

Compliant Child Victim
The compliance of children should not matter, but often does.

The dynamics of *compliant child victims* became another important but unpopular topic, that based on my growing experience and insight, I felt compelled to speak about. I have written several articles, given many presentations, and testified numerous times in court about compliant child victims. I did so because so many people fail to recognize or understand the concept. It isn't considered politically correct, but I saw how cases involving this type of behavior caused problems for investigators, prosecutors, and the victims.

Colleagues told me I shouldn't talk about compliant victims because the consent of children does not matter. If true, why were so many people upset when I talked about victims cooperating? Why

LOVE, BOMBS, AND MOLESTERS 117

did so many prosecutors ask me to educate the court about it? My educational testimony was less about the legal significance of the consent or compliance but more about how it affects victim behavior.

The consent of children shouldn't matter, but to many it does. Victims often feel shame, guilt, and embarrassment over their compliance. As a result, they sometimes accurately report they were sexually victimized but inaccurately report the details of how they were victimized. They make a valid allegation of abuse that includes false details of how it happened. Many professionals and non-professionals alike have an overwhelming need to believe that sexual activity between adults and children is always unwanted by the child. That may usually be true but it is not always true, especially when dealing with adolescent children.

The difference between what we say and what we truly think was illustrated by the response to a 2005 civil lawsuit when I testified about the sexual victimization of an adolescent boy. Attorneys for one large, youth-serving organization filed a motion stating, "Children forcibly abused and threatened with harm if they tell are victims. His consent, as a matter of law, to sexual contacts bars his claims. The [organization] has no duty to investigate and police the private life of any teenage member who chooses to become involved in a **consensual** (emphasis added) relationship with an adult volunteer."

Even if civil law supported such a legal position, did the organization communicate that attitude beforehand to the parents who put their children in that organization's care? Did the prevention and public relations material used by the organization reflect that position or did it state that such activity is never the fault of the child? Many simply do not understand the reality of compliant child victims.

Age of Consent
Consent for what, with whom?

The fundamental legal difference between sexual victimization of adults and that of children is not that children are smaller or more innocent. The issue is one of consent. With sexual activity between adults, with a few rare exceptions, there must be a lack of consent in order for it to be a crime. Even with adults, the concept of consent is sometimes uncertain. It can range from a definitive "no" with resistance to a specific "yes" to each act and be complicated by issues such as nonverbal communication and unequal power relationships. Successful prosecution, however, usually depends on being able to prove lack of consent or inability to give it – such as when a victim is incompetent or incapacitated from drugs or alcohol. With sexual activity between children and adults, a crime can occur even if the child cooperates. Successful prosecution usually does not involve having to prove lack of consent. The reason we protect children and don't recognize their legal consent to have sex with adults is not because they are innocent, but because they are developmentally immature (*e.g.,* brain development, cognitive decision-making, judgment). It is wrong and counterproductive to inflict on children this burden of heroic innocence.

Why then do we so often want to apply the adult standard to child victim cases? I believe the answer is rooted in the need to believe.

The reality about the age of consent is not so simple. Age of consent can vary, depending on the type of sexual activity and individuals involved. The age at which a child can engage in sexual activity, consent to get married, appear in pornography, or leave home without parental permission to have sex with an unrelated adult varies. Throughout U.S. history large numbers of individuals younger than eighteen have legally gotten married. Federal case law seems to suggest the consent of a fourteen-year-old, who crosses state lines after running off and having sex with a forty-year-old man she met online, may not be a valid defense for a sexual assault charge. But it could be a valid defense for a kidnapping charge. In the U.S., when an adult and a child have sex under compliant circumstances, under the standards of the criminal law and the norms of most of the population, the adult is **always** the offender and the child is **always** the victim.

But who is a child under the standards? As this is being written, in France (a modern, Western, industrialized, democracy) a bill is being drafted to set for the first time a legal age for sexual consent. The bill would say that sex with children under a certain age is by definition coercive. At what age can there be no concept of consent? There is apparently disagreement, with the ages thirteen and fifteen seeming to be the most discussed.

Nice Guy Offenders
Some child molesters don't just appear to be nice, they are nice.

Cases involving nice-guy offenders who seem to love and are often loved by children are especially problematic. People object when I say, "the offender was a nice guy." They'd prefer I say something like "the offender seemed like a nice guy." Many do not understand that pedophiles are merely individuals with a sexual preference for children. That preference says little or nothing about the other aspects of their character and personality. Because most people find child sexual abuse to be offensive and repulsive, they believe that people who do it must be offensive and repulsive. Some are, but many are not.

Over and over, I observed that pedophiles were not being recognized, investigated, charged, convicted, or sent to prison simply because they were or were perceived to be, nice guys. Even today, media and society still view it as a contradiction when someone is a caring, honored teacher (clergy member, coach, doctor, children's volunteer) and is sexually victimizing a child in their care.

The vast majority of dedicated schoolteachers are not pedophiles, but many pedophiles who become schoolteachers are decorated teachers. Being nice has little to do with being a child molester. But it does increase the likelihood of getting away with the crime long enough to repeat it many times. This is why it's crucial for us to recognize that some molesters are also "nice guys." Determining or verifying that someone is a nice guy cannot be the sole basis for concluding an allegation is false or unfounded.

Grooming/Seduction
No great mystery; with adults it's called dating.

In this context, the term *grooming* refers to specific nonviolent techniques used by some child molesters to gain access to and control of their child victims. There is an old joke that says the definition of an expert is a guy from a thousand miles away with a briefcase. Many times prosecutors have asked me to travel to their jurisdiction as an expert witness, to explain the dynamics of grooming to a jury. It's as if they need to bring in a consultant from far away with special knowledge to explain some obscure process known only to a few experts. When I do testify, I quickly try to make it clear that the technique itself is no great mystery.

Everyone on the jury knows in general what sexual grooming or seduction is. The only difference for each of them is how long ago it was since someone did it to them or they did it to someone else. For some of them, I say, it may have been the night before. For me, it was during the long ago days when I wanted to get married, at the beginning of my Navy career. It is its application to victimization of children that is poorly understood. People have a problem imagining that something done by typical adults in a sexual relationship is in any way related to something done by a child molester and child victim in a sexual relationship. When an adult is groomed, any resulting sexual activity is ordinarily not a crime. When a child is groomed, any resulting sexual activity ordinarily is a crime.

The repeated use of terms such as *rape* and *sexual violence* when discussing or inquiring about the sexual victimization of children assumes or implies in the minds of many that all real child victims resist sexual advances by adults; are then overpowered by coercion, trickery, threats, weapons, or physical force; and then report it the first chance they can. Offenders with reasonably good interpersonal skills can usually control children without resorting to threats or use of violence.

Grooming and seducing child victims without the use of violence typically involves the most effective combination of attention, affection, kindness, privileges, recognition, fun events, gifts, alcohol, drugs, or money. This is done until the victims' inhibitions are lowered and their cooperation and willingness is gained. The exact nature of this seduction depends, in part, on the developmental stages, needs, and vulnerabilities of each targeted child, and the nature of that child's relationship with the offender. The skilled offender adjusts his methods to fit the targeted child. Child molesters who have an acquaintance relationship with their victims are the most likely to use such techniques and to be nonviolent. To assist with their access to and control of children, offenders often use related grooming techniques with parents, guardians, caretakers, and youth-serving organizations. Some grooming/seduction activities – affection, touching, hugging, massaging – can also provide sexual gratification for the offender and may even constitute sex offenses by themselves. Grooming activity is not always just a prelude to sex but can be sex.

Acquaintance Child Molesters
The forgotten child molester – he is one of us.

Because of the potential sexual interest of many heterosexual men in teenage girls, society generally limits their access to such girls in a variety of ways. For example, an adult man would generally not be allowed to shower or bathe with, use the same rest room as, sleep or change clothing in front of, or take these girls unchaperoned on overnight trips. They certainly *would be* allowed to interact with them publically in many ways such as teaching them in school, religiously ministering to them, working with them, and helping them.

While I was in high school, Father Quinn, my priest and coach, took me and three or four other adolescent boys on the swimming team to the National Catholic Interscholastic Swimming Championships being held at Villanova University. He drove us from the Bronx, New York, to Philadelphia, Pennsylvania. We spent several nights there, sleeping on cots in the hallways of a school gymnasium. We competed in the big swim meet and then he drove us all home. There were no other parents or chaperones with us on this trip. It was one of the highlights of my swimming career and nothing inappropriate or sexual happened.

At the time, neither my parents nor I recognized the potential risks involved in that overnight trip. Even back then, however, I doubt this male priest would have been allowed to do the same with a group of adolescent girls. As a result of my later work, I came to realize the overnight trip was a high-risk situation. Fortunately for me, the priest had no such sexual interest in me and was an inspirational and positive role model in my life. That does not mean, however, that we should not recognize the potential risks in such activity and take appropriate precautions. Especially since in 2014, I learned that Father Quinn did have a sexual interest in children, but unlike most child molesting priests it was for girls, not boys.

That chance gender preference may have saved me from sexual victimization as a young boy. And when appropriate in my presentations, I used my experience with Father Quinn to emphasize the teaching point that child molesters can appear to be and often are nice guys. It is difficult for me, because each time I spoke of it, my eyes would tear up and my voice would choke a little. But the teaching point was important. This priest was one of the nicest and most influential individuals in my life – and yet he apparently, since he was never convicted, was a child molester.

Youth-Serving Organizations
Provide not just access but also validation.

Youth-serving organizations satisfy an instrumental need of acquaintance child molesters to gain access to potential victims, and a psychological need to justify and validate their behavior as worthwhile (*see* Appendix III, Lanning & Dietz, 2014). Officials in youth-serving organizations often know something inappropriate is happening but rarely understand its full significance. The offenders and victims in these cases seldom fit society's preferred stereotypes. Administrators and other personnel often have no concept of nice guys repeatedly grooming compliant adolescent victims within a respected youth-serving organization. They are, in fact, looking for an evil predator and their employee or volunteer doesn't look or appear evil. As mentioned earlier, part of the problem is the common label, *predator*, for such offenders. This label interferes with the ability to recognize them. How do you explain him being an effective coach and doing charitable work to help children? This guy must somehow be different or atypical. Is showering with boys or giving them back rubs "weird" "creepy" "icky" or sexual activity? The details of such activity are usually avoided as awkward and unpleasant.

Do they even recognize what is happening in front of them? So just what is the difference between mentoring and grooming? If he victimized so many children, why didn't they all immediately report it? Since so few victims have come forward, how could they be innocent child victims? These are the questions people ask when they don't understand this type of case. That makes it easier to minimize or dismiss victims who don't disclose their abuse, or who appear to be cooperating in their own victimization.

Where was the report from the boy allegedly seen being victimized in the shower at Penn State? The 2011 Penn State University case is a significant example of such cases. It also summarizes many of these poorly understood dynamics. Obviously, there should be some recourse for the victims of any negligence by such organizations. Other than the criminal conviction of the offender, this ordinarily takes the form of monetary payment as part of a civil judgment. It could also include some assurance that policies and procedures will change. Because the Penn State case involved former and current members of their athletic department, the NCAA also got involved. They ultimately decided to impose major sanctions on the University's football program, including vacating wins from 1998-2011, the loss of scholarships, and a four-year ban from postseason games. Many child advocates I've worked with over the years applauded and supported these sanctions.

I won't speculate about the reasons for this decision and the support for it. It makes little sense to me, however, for the NCAA to directly punish the competitive football program for the unrelated actions of the University's coaches and administrators. This is like a Catholic bishop limiting several years of the religious services at the parish of a sex-offending priest, and declaring null and void all recent confessions and weddings conducted by him and his superiors. I know that many people will disagree with this opinion and analogy because they believe that the failures of the University were directly linked to and caused by its revered football program.

Some of the sanctions have since been removed.

Based on my experience with hundreds of similar cases, however, this explanation is too simplistic and self-serving. I agree that the desire to avoid negative, organizational publicity was a major factor in the case but the same failures regularly happen in many other youth-serving organizations. Wanting to protect your reputation is not unique to universities with successful football programs. The bigger the reputation, the greater the need to protect it. And the greater likelihood the administration might be tempted to try varying degrees of damage control. The specific area or basis for the outstanding reputation in question matters little. This tendency seems to be reduced in less prestigious organizations. In my work, I discovered that the failure of youth-serving organizations to adequately respond in protecting children is usually the result of some complex **combination** of a variety of inadvertent and intentional reasons that seem to affect the judgment of the decision makers. Of these, ignorance and damage control seem to be the most dominant.

If Penn State had put as much effort into learning about this problem as they put into ensuring compliance with NCAA sports regulations, they might have both recognized **and** understood what was happening. Simplistically blaming football punishes innocent bystanders and makes it easier for other types of youth-serving organizations to continue improperly addressing the same problem.

And if protecting their football program was the cause, why do so many youth-serving organizations do the same thing? To me, the NCAA response is mostly another example of the issue being driven primarily by politics and emotion – rather than professional analysis and objectivity. Big-time college football has as much to do with what happened at Penn State, as gun control has to do with what happened in Aurora, Colorado or Newtown, Connecticut.

Throughout my FBI career, I learned that most complex human behavior has multiple causes, motivations, or factors. After retiring from the FBI, I was retained as an expert in many civil cases involving the sexual victimization of children. Because civil lawsuits are about money, the suit is usually against someone with deep pockets – a youth-serving organization. Working for both plaintiff and defendant attorneys, I identified many reasons why youth-serving organizations do such a bad job in this area. I eventually concluded that no one of these reasons explains all cases and most cases involve some combination of more than one of them. One motivation also does not preclude others. I also believe that another significant factor in some cases is the difficulty a young or lower-level employee might have in discussing the details of observed or suspected deviant sexual behavior with a powerful and straight-laced older administrator. To properly analyze and evaluate these cases you need details. However, to paraphrase the movie *A Few Good Men*, people can't handle the truth. They often prefer to make decisions without knowing the details – which repulse and offend them.

Over the years I have been repeatedly asked how so many acquaintance offenders get away with molesting so many children so many times for so long. Why would a child not report hundreds of incidents of molestations by a known offender who is not a family member? To effectively recognize, intervene, and prevent sexual molestation within youth-serving organizations by acquaintance sex offenders who gain access to and control of children in the context of their occupations and volunteer work, responsible adults must understand and address four interrelated but commonly misunderstood phenomena: (1) the diversity of what could be sexual activity, (2) "nice guy" offenders, (3) compliant child victims, and (4) the grooming/seduction process. Organizations must often deal with difficult cases in which well-liked individuals who are dedicated to helping children sexually victimize children over time in ways that may involve behavior generally not thought of as sexual (e.g., touching, hugging, massaging, examining, horse play, etc.); children are controlled through a grooming/seduction process (e.g., providing attention, affection, privileges, recognition, fun events, gifts, money, drugs, alcohol, etc.) rather than the threat or use of force or violence; and child victims often cooperate in, deny, or do not report their victimization, and may even support and defend the offender.

During the late 1980s and 1990s, while I was still in the FBI, various youth-serving organizations contacted me. They asked about children in their care being sexually victimized by their workers, and how best to respond, as well as address civil litigation issues. I gave them general information and shared my research findings, but I couldn't officially get involved in civil cases then. However, many of these organizations used my publications as part of their efforts to address the problem.

After I retired from the FBI in 2000, I got more involved with the issue and was retained as an expert in many civil cases. In 2007, I spoke about child pornography for the U.S. Conference of Catholic Bishops, at the "Promise to Protect" seminar in Washington, DC. I mentioned my Catholic education at St. Nicholas of Tolentine in the Bronx. When the seminar was over, a Dominican nun from Blauvelt, who had been in the audience, told me she knew Sister Evelyn, my teacher in the sixth and seventh grades who was sure I was going to be a priest.

Just the mention of Sister Evelyn's name meant a lot to me, because she was such an important influence in my life. Although I wonder what she'd think if she knew that instead of becoming a priest, I lecture about child pornography.

Chapter Seven
"Say No, Yell, and Tell"

In addressing and preventing stranger-danger cases, the advice was thought to be fairly straightforward. Children were told the kind of things contained in an old FBI produced coloring page that agents formerly distributed, such as: "For your protection, remember to turn down gifts from strangers, and refuse rides offered by strangers." The images on this page portrayed a clear contrast between the evil of the offender and the goodness of the potential child victim. To help identify a potential abductor, children were often told things such as "adults don't ask children for directions." When confronted with such an offender, the advice to the child is simple and clear – *"say no, yell, and tell"* or "recognize, resist, and report."

My growing insight and analysis of the sexual victimization of children also affected my views on many prevention efforts. More detail and context on this topic is contained in the 5th edition (2010) of my monograph titled *Child Molesters: A Behavioral Analysis for Professionals Investigating the Sexual Exploitation of Children* (*see* Appendix III).

As previously discussed, the relationship between adult sex offenders and their child victims plays a significant role in the methods offenders use to access and control their victims. A simple way for both investigators and nonprofessionals to understand these important variations is to divide these relationships into three useful categories: *stranger*, *intrafamilial*, and *acquaintance*. These categories can be difficult to precisely define, especially when it comes to children. So they are best viewed on a relational continuum. Understanding the methods of access and control used by offenders is essential to developing effective prevention strategies.

Many adults love to reminisce about an idealistic childhood, a time they didn't lock their doors and went out to play with no fear of abduction. Those same adults today believe they cannot let their children out of their sight. This has recently resulted in sensitive arguments about "helicopter parents" who monitor their children's every move and "free range parents" who allow their children the freedom to learn how to be independent. No parents like to be accused of improperly protecting their children. And until recently, my grandson was never on a school day trip that his mother, my daughter, did not find a reason to join him.

My parents were more of the "free range" style. When growing up in the Bronx, I was allowed to cross increasingly "bigger" streets and move further from my home on my own, the older I became. By the time I was thirteen, I rode my bicycle about five miles south to Yankee Stadium for a 1957 World Series day game between the New York Yankees and the Milwaukee Braves. Soon I rode about twenty miles north to Tarrytown, New York. My parents' only rule? To be home by 6:00 p.m. for supper.

Much of the time, my parents had no idea exactly where I was. Did that make me a missing child? By some definitions, the answer is yes. In reality, the answer is no. And in fairness to my parents, I think over time I earned their trust and that freedom. I am sure many would disagree.

Current best estimates place nonfamily abductions at about 105 children every year. These abductions fit our stereotypical image of an abducted **and** missing child. The very real danger of sexual victimization for children comes predominately from family members and acquaintances, **not strangers**.

Remember that my parents allowed me to go with a priest unchaperoned on an overnight trip. Concerning sexual victimization, that was probably riskier than allowing me to freely roam my neighborhood. But it doesn't mean that stereotypical child abductions are just folklore. Strangers still use lures, like candy or faking a need for help, to successfully abduct children. Those cases, though, are the exception rather than the rule.

A few years ago Kathy and I were driving in an unfamiliar area of central Virginia. As we drove, I realized the car was almost out of gas. As usual, and like most husbands, I explained to Kathy that we weren't lost – I just didn't know where I was. We weren't in the wilderness of Montana, and there had to be a nearby gas station. When we came to a "T" intersection, I wanted to turn toward the nearest gas station. But I didn't know if a left turn or a right turn would accomplish that. Just then I saw a young adolescent boy beside the road.

He probably knows the direction of the nearest gas station, I thought. As I rolled down my window to ask, the prevention advice I had heard many times, "Adults don't ask children for directions," suddenly popped into my head.

But that's not right, I thought. While I would certainly never ask the boy to stand next to me or get in my car, what was so unusual or menacing to simply ask if he knew the direction of the nearest gas station?

That train of thought led me to remember many occasions during my own childhood when adults asked me for directions. For example, when my family used to vacation in the Catskill Mountains in upstate New York, there was a small town spelled C-a-i-r-o as the city in Egypt. But the locals pronounced it "Karo" as in the syrup. Strangers driving by would frequently ask for directions to "Cairo." I remember this because most of them said it the way you pronounce the city in Egypt. We gave them directions, but after they left, my friends and I would make a joke about them finding their way to Egypt. I realized I had blindly accepted as prevention gospel a statement that was not essentially accurate. It sounded like it was accurate information, but it wasn't. Certainly, not all the time. I decided that such convoluted advice must be confusing to children.

Another difficulty with prevention advice targeted for a mass audience is knowing how to address variations in the targeted children. Age and gender variations can be important, but are more easily addressed. Individual variations in development and personality are more difficult. My wife and I raised two children – a girl and a boy. They were as different as night and day. My daughter was shy and introverted. My son was outgoing and extroverted. We never had to tell my daughter to not talk to strangers. We had to tell her to talk to her relatives.

During my assignments in the Navy and FBI, we lived away from our extended family members. From my young daughter's perspective, her grandmother was a stranger. My daughter was just naturally cautious and uncomfortable with people she didn't know well. We had to tell her to say hello to and hug her grandmother. Did she have the right to say no?

Our son would talk to anyone at anytime. He even took great delight in hiding in the clothes racks when shopping with his mother and then testing her patience by jumping out just as her fear that he had been abducted reached a frenzy. Some kids will talk to every stranger they meet no matter what you tell them. Obviously, prevention efforts should be modified to some degree for varying types of children.

Contrary to popular belief, the best available research tells us that the vast majority of children abducted by nonfamily members are released relatively unharmed a short time later. In spite of what the research indicates, it's now almost universally recommended that children confronting potential abductors should always resist and fight. This might result in some children not being abducted. But the research findings should be a caution about such universal advice. Resistance could result in children becoming one of the one percent of abducted children murdered or severely injured – instead of the ninety-nine percent released relatively unharmed. The child who gets away by resisting can go on television and tell his or her story for everyone to hear. The child who gets murdered or severely injured as a result of resisting cannot.

Giving advice to avoid abduction situations is easier than giving confrontation advice when avoidance did not work. Confrontation advice is a complex and difficult decision that should be based on hard-to-know factors such as the type of offender, the personality of the child, and the location of the attempted abduction. I am not suggesting that children should never actively resist, but the research findings need to be objectively evaluated and considered before arbitrarily doling out simplistic advice that may make the situation worse.

Are all children capable of effectively resisting in high-stress situations? Some children will comply with almost any command sternly given to them by a powerful adult. I would like to believe I know what I'd do if confronted with an abductor. But since it has never happened, I really don't know for sure.

In the 1980s, I was assigned as the BSU agent to consult on an FBI investigation involving a sexually sadistic serial killer who was responsible for abducting and murdering a dozen or more victims. His sexual preference was for very attractive young women many of whom he lured to their deaths. His ruse? He promised to photograph them and help them become fashion models. Three of his abducted victims survived. One woman he abducted survived by screaming and fighting while he held her captive in a motel room. She was able to get free, run outside, and attract attention. He then fled the scene. After being identified, he was placed on the FBI Ten Most Wanted List. However, he continued to abduct, torture, and murder victims. Through his crime spree, the FBI tracked him as he traveled back and forth across the country.

He then lured and abducted a fifteen-year-old girl on the West Coast. Although an adolescent child, like all his other victims she was an attractive, mature-looking female. He tortured her, but she did not respond as his other victims had. She did not fulfill his sexual fantasies and expectations. As a result, their relationship gradually changed as they traveled 3,000 miles across the country. He eventually bought her a ticket, put her on a plane, and sent her back home. The third victim survived by sheer will power, playing dead after he left her severely injured by the side of a road. After he drove away, she crawled onto the road and was rescued by a passerby. That serial killer later died in a shootout with the police. Three of his many victims survived, but each one as a result of a totally different response. What specific confrontation advice would you then give to potential victims of such an offender?

Even the classic avoidance advice, "never leave your children unattended" seems difficult to apply to the eighty-one percent of child abduction victims who are teenagers. I doubt that most parents truly understand that fingerprinting, photographing, and collecting DNA from their child, although probably not a bad idea, in no way reduces the risk the child will be abducted or run away. Most likely, those parents are not even considering the runaway possibility. Photographs and video may help locate the child and fingerprints and DNA may help with positive identification. Yet, no one wants to tell the parents at the child identification program that the fingerprints and DNA being taken are most useful if their children are found dead or refuse to accurately identify themselves because they don't want to return home. Parents would rather believe they are somehow protecting their children.

So why then do so many people believe that the abduction of children by sexual predators is more common than it actually is? That programs to fingerprint children are effective prevention strategies? Or that a "yucky" feeling identifies sexual abuse? There are many possible answers, but I have given you the most significant one I uncovered. It's the same reason so many well-intentioned individuals (as opposed to unethical con artists) trying to prevent sexual victimization distort and exaggerate facts, deceive themselves, appeal to emotion, make errors in judgment, and believe they are objective, when they are not. It is, as I learned so well, that adults tend to believe what they want or need to believe—the greater the need, the greater the tendency.

When it was widely recognized that children are most often sexually victimized by people they know, prevention advice became more complicated. Consequently, prevention programs were developed based on more complex concepts such as good touching and bad touching, the *yucky* feeling, and a child's right to say no. These are not the kinds of things easily and effectively communicated in fifty minutes to hundreds of kids of varying ages packed into a school auditorium. These are challenging issues, and prevention programs need to be carefully developed and evaluated. Sometimes bad touches feel good and good touches feel bad. What does it mean to get the *yucky* feeling?

I thought about my early childhood in the Bronx. My grandparents, Nanny and Pop Pop, lived two floors up in our apartment building. On Sunday evenings we often had dinner with them. As my three sisters and I walked up the two flights of stairs, we invariably asked our parents, "Do we have to kiss Pop Pop?"

There were two reasons we did not want to kiss Pop Pop. First, he often did not shave on the weekend. By Sunday night the stubble on his face burned when he affectionately rubbed it against our faces. (I later told my family I had genetically inherited his trait of not shaving on the weekend.) Second, after kissing us, Pop Pop loved to affectionately pinch our cheeks.

Of course back then no child had the right to say no. My parents said Pop Pop loved us, and we had to kiss him. But if I heard a school presentation about good touch/bad touch, come Monday morning, I might have reported that kiss and pinch as bad touches. I can only hope that had this happened, an unbiased, well-trained professional would have objectively evaluated the matter. They certainly gave me a "yucky" feeling, but they weren't sexual abuse.

Over the years, parents have often asked for my advice about how to protect their children from sexual victimization. While I am certainly not an expert on the most effective ways to communicate with children, I do know something about *how* these crimes are committed. Nonetheless, my responses usually shock them.

"If you or a family member is sexually abusing your children stop it and get help," I say first. This advice is based on statistical probabilities. They usually quickly assure me that is not the case. I then tell them that after a family member, their child is next, and most likely, to be sexually victimized by an acquaintance. If their children are young, whenever possible they must assume the child care responsibility for their children. Each time they put their child in the hands of someone else, there is a risk. They usually then tell me things like they have to work, or need time for themselves, or have to send their children to daycare or school. I remind them that I said "whenever possible," not "always."

I then share something imprecise with them, which I first heard many years ago. While it's about protecting yourself from fraud, it certainly applied to child sexual abuse. Because the old adage, "If it sounds too good to be true, maybe it is," may apply here. If someone's interest in children seems too good to be true, maybe it is. This is not proof that someone is a child molester, but it is a reason to be alert or suspicious. This adage becomes more significant when this excessive interest is combined with other indicators. Be less concerned about adults excessively interested in all children. Be more concerned about those excessively interested in either boys or girls of very specific ages. So beware, parents, of anyone who wants to be with your children more than you do.

Why would any parent put their child in the hands of someone who seems too good to be true? Sometimes, they have few other options. I hope by now you are beginning to understand the most likely and significant answer – the need to believe that nice people who like their children and offer to help them could not possibly be child molesters.

Years ago, in one of the cases on which I was consulting, the investigators recovered materials that some offenders often use to rationalize and validate their sexual interest in children. They found it in the home of a child molester. Although it represents how many of them want or need to think of themselves, it can be useful when trying to identify such offenders. The offender's material said that if children want to identify him and other "child lovers," their distinguishing traits are that: "they will smile at you, they will try to make you laugh or be happy, they will enjoy being with you, they will like to sit right next to you, they will like to hold your hand, they will give you candy – but not before dinner, they will like to share enjoyable things with you, they will want to make you feel good – all over, they will love you, and they will want you to love them." Although there is clearly an element of self-serving rationalization in this material, this is exactly how children, parents, and society will perceive some of these molesters.

This means advice designed to prevent the sexual victimization of children by adult acquaintances is even more complex and challenging to implement. How do you warn children about molesters who may be their teacher, coach, clergy member, therapist, or social media best friend forever? Whose only distinguishing characteristics are they will treat the children better than most adults, listen to their problems and concerns, and fill their emotional, physical, and sexual needs? Will families, society, and professionals understand when the victimization is suspected, discovered, or disclosed? Maybe, but maybe not.

A great deal of the prevention advice simply doesn't distinguish the types of sexual victimization it applies to. Simplistic advice advocating, "Say no, yell and tell" or "Recognize, resist and report" may reflect our hope as parents. But it's likely to have little impact on cases involving acquaintance molesters, who effectively groom or seduce their compliant child victims. It also may increase feelings of guilt in children who don't follow the advice. And remember, the right to say no would apply differently to a stranger, family member, teacher, or coach.

It seems to me that telling a child they have the right to say no to an adult implies they also have the right to say yes. Many people assume children would always say no, when it comes to engaging in sexual activity with an adult. In addition, having told the child they have the right to say no, I have never met a parent who then actually grants that right to the child in many situations.

Without explaining the distinctions, and like me with my Pop Pop, parents make their children do things they don't want to do all the time. Most people don't realize that some better-educated and more intelligent child molesters actually base part of the rationalization for their behavior on the concept that children should have the right to choose their sexual partners.

In my opinion, children don't have the right to say either no or yes, because they are developmentally immature. Certain adults also may have the right to touch them against their will in situations involving health and safety; however, some offenders might use such situations to sexually exploit them. These complexities are one reason I have a fundamental problem with putting too much prevention responsibility on children.

Next, I tell parents to see if the youth-serving organizations (schools, churches, sports, camp, scouting) in which their children participate have programs to screen and supervise employees and volunteers and specific plans about how to respond to suspicions, allegations, and complaints. I tell them to check on the organization's history with such issues. Parents need to be especially cautious about certain high-risk situations. For instance, a skilled child molester who can get children into a situation where they must change clothing or stay with him overnight will frequently succeed in seducing and victimizing them.

I also point out the differences between trying to protect young children and trying to protect adolescent children. Almost all children seek attention and affection. Children, especially adolescents, are often interested in and curious about sexuality and sexually explicit material. They often engage in high-risk behavior without considering or comprehending the consequences. Typically, children younger than twelve tend to listen to prevention advice, but often do not understand it. Children older than twelve tend to understand it, but often no longer listen. When a young adolescent girl was asked on a television program if she followed the rules her parents set for her safety, she responded that she often didn't, because "rules are made to be broken."

There are also far more men sexually interested in pubescent teenage children than in prepubescent young children. The vast majority of men can be sexually stimulated by the physical appearance of pubescent children, but most don't act on these urges. There are many reasons, however, why an adult might have sex with an adolescent child. They range from a long-term sexual preference to situational dynamics, such as the forbidden nature makes it exciting, it brings back memories of their less stressful adolescent years, adolescents are less judgmental or threatening, and adolescents are less likely to have sexually transmitted diseases.

Children, especially boys, typically find pornography online because they are looking for it – not because they made a mistake or inadvertently stumbled upon it. They are moving away from the total control of parents and trying to establish new relationships outside the family. Ask any adult man what was the number one thing on their mind when they were adolescents. The answer is always the same: sex. During my adolescent years in the Bronx, my friends and I spent many hours searching for sexually explicit pictures among the discarded magazines stored in the basement of my apartment building until garbage pick-up day. Back then, we felt lucky if we found some underwear ads in a store catalog or nude natives in the *National Geographic* magazine. The fundamental sexual urge is the same, but with today's Internet technology, an adolescent exploring his or her sexuality can find the most extreme pornography ever created. Yet, many parents seem to want to believe their children are asexual and, I suppose, many children want to believe the same of their parents.

It's far easier to prevent things that both the parent and child don't want to happen, such as forced sex with a sadistic sexual predator you met online. It's harder to prevent things the parent does not want to happen, but the child does, such as romantic sex or a good time with an exciting, good-looking adult friend you met online. From the potential child victim's perspective, the typical online offender is **less** like the stranger in the playground and **more** like the nice acquaintance who lives in the neighborhood. Children are bombarded all day long with commercials for online sites promising you can find the love of your life or your soul mate. Social media has redefined what it means to be a friend, as well as turned the word into a verb.

To paraphrase comedian Jimmy Kimmel, a real friend is someone you invite to your house for Thanksgiving dinner; nobody has 5,000 friends. Even the term *like* has new meaning. Parents also need to recognize the problem of asking your children to "do as I say, not as I do." It is hard to expect children to abide by rules for online safety when parents download pornography and disclose private information, exchange explicit photographs, and travel to meet an online stranger.

Some prevention material dealing with online child safety still only warns about not talking to strangers or predators. It advises children to tell their parents if someone they meet online makes them feel scared, confused, or uncomfortable. It's unrealistic or even inaccurate to suggest that someone you regularly communicate with for weeks or months is a stranger just because you have not met him or her in person. Many online offenders are reasonably honest about their identity and some even send recognizable photographs of themselves. They spend hours, days, weeks, and months communicating, including a lot of listening, with children.

So warning potential victims about online predators can communicate a false impression of the nature of the danger. Research tells us that in most cases where adolescents have left home to personally meet adults they first met online; they did so voluntarily, in the hope they were going to have sex (as opposed to getting help with their homework) with someone they believed they knew and who cared about them. Adolescent children are unlikely to tell about sexual contacts and solicitations when they perceive this activity to be fun, adventurous, or desirable.

I usually conclude with something that is easy for me to say – but very hard for any parent to do. I tell them that protecting or making their children safer is less about hardware, software, and dire warnings about predators. Instead, it's more about being involved in their lives, communication (including about sex), and love. Strive for the kind of relationship that might allow your child to tell you he did something he was not supposed to do. What are the odds their adolescent son would tell them about the thousands of pornographic images he downloaded with his new computer before he received the bizarre ones that now make him feel *uncomfortable*? What would their reaction be if their son did tell them? If parents' efforts don't totally prevent sexual victimization, they may at least minimize how often it happens and for how long. Remember relationships with acquaintance offenders are usually ongoing.

I also know that many people, either by nature or choice, live in a world of denial. In my current neighborhood, thefts of valuables from unlocked cars parked on the driveway are common. I personally find it hard to believe that anyone would leave valuables in their car much less not lock the car. And some people don't even lock the doors to their house. This is beyond comprehension for someone like me, who was born and raised in New York City and spent thirty years in law enforcement. On the other hand, there are helicopter parents who never let their children out of their sight. Parents must strike a balance between denial and paranoia.

Some people have asked me about sex-offender registration and community notification but I won't discuss that here in any detail. Quite simply, I believe that sex-offender registration should be offender-based – not offense-based. That is, it should be based on an analysis and evaluation of the totality of the specific offender's background and behavior patterns, not simply on the specific violation he was convicted for. I say this because the offense an offender is technically found or pleads guilty to may not truly reflect the danger and real risk level. In addition, if we're going to restrict the activities of registered sex offenders, sufficient funds should be appropriated for the needed resources to monitor them for compliance.

In this chapter, I've pointed out some realistic and relevant dynamics to consider and incorporated into preventing the sexual victimization of children. I have especially tried to provide insight into the relatively common, but poorly understood, problem of child sexual victimization by acquaintance offenders – the forgotten child molester.

CHAPTER EIGHT
"NY DR 1-102"

During my work with sexually victimized children, I learned that many child molesters, especially those I considered preferential sex offenders in my typology, spend their lives trying to convince themselves they are not immoral sexual deviants or criminals. They prefer to believe they are high-minded, loving individuals whose behavior is misunderstood, or simply politically incorrect at this particular time in history. When they refer to themselves, it's as "boy lovers" or "child lovers" – but not child molesters.

As I view it, *rationalization* usually involves convincing themselves or others that their sexual activity with children is not harmful. *Validation* includes convincing themselves or others that their sexual activity with children is actually beneficial. This is not uncommon. Child molesters frequently try to justify their behavior to others. They might claim they care for children more than the children's parents do, and say what they do is good for the children. Many child molesters simply do not believe that having sex with children constitutes molesting or hurting them. A response that they did not "molest" a child or would "never hurt a child" can be sincere but *not* necessarily a denial that they had sex with a child.

Their efforts to justify their behavior often center on blaming the victim. Some offenders go into great detail explaining the difference between consenting and forced sex with children. **But such justification should have no meaning**. A crime was still committed. Again, the major legal difference between sex crimes committed against children and adults is this: with child victims consent should not matter.

That's why some of the more clever child molesters come up with ingenious stories to explain their behavior. Admitting some alleged acts – while denying their intent was sexual – is very common.

Many sex offenders who victimize children within their family claim to be providing sex education. Such stories work even better for an acquaintance molester who is a professional, such as a clergy member, teacher, coach, doctor, or therapist. Even when not professionals, acquaintance offenders still come up with inventive claims about the reason for their questionable behavior.

A wide variety of individuals use a wide variety of rationalizations to justify a wide variety of behaviors. I eventually came to believe that the rationalizations used by many child molesters to justify sex with children is surpassed in absurdity, ardency, and audacity only by those used by defense attorneys to justify helping to get factually and obviously guilty individuals acquitted. There is a difference between factual guilt – what the defendant actually did and legal guilt – what the prosecutor can actually prove. You have to be clever and resourceful to be able to validate deliberate deceitful behavior by claiming it is actually principled.

Defending guilty people is a constitutional right and obviously not a crime. People are presumed innocent until they are legally declared guilty in a court of law, even if they confess. I'm not suggesting that this behavior by defense attorneys is like, or worse than, that of child molesters. I am suggesting, though, that the rationalization and validation for legally defending clearly and obviously guilty criminals is more pervasive and sophisticated. No doubt my opinion will outrage and offend most attorneys. They will argue I am ignorant and biased about the law. I am fully aware of the explanations defense attorneys use to justify such actions. But as with the diverse rationalizations of child molesters, they do not convince me. The factual guilt of some offenders can be known with certainty and they deserve to be convicted.

Since 1990, my favorite television program has been the original *Law & Order* series. When I was growing up, we only got about six channels on our television. Now I get several hundred channels on my cable system – I am not yet into streaming. Probably because I am old, it seems there were more good things to watch on the six channels of my youth than on the three hundred channels of my old age. Many nights I channel surf for hours trying to find anything worthwhile to watch. Reality television seems to be just scripted television using amateur actors or washed up celebrities to display bad behavior. Most of the time I wind up watching sports, the History Channel, *Pardon the Interruption* (*PTI*), *Blue Bloods*, or reruns of *Law & Order*.

This is where being old really pays off. It usually takes me about forty minutes to realize I have seen a particular *Law & Order* episode before and then another fifteen to remember the ending. By the time the show ends, I got to enjoy it all over again.

The main reason I enjoy watching *Law & Order* is not because of its accuracy. It's more because the show portrays the investigation and prosecution of criminal cases in a complex and balanced way. The show tells an interesting and entertaining crime story, complete with a twist at the end, while making you think about a variety of important issues. Intelligent characters use intelligent arguments to express differing and dissenting points of view. I'm sure that the writers and producers have their own personal perspectives, but they put words in the mouths of intelligent characters who express alternative, compelling, and diverse views.

For example, in late 2009 I watched a *Law & Order* episode about the murder of a doctor who performed late-term abortions. It was, without a doubt, the most balanced, thought-provoking, and intelligent program on the topic of abortion I ever saw. In that one-hour, entertaining, fictional episode, all the complex issues involving abortion were presented, argued, debated, and discussed by the program's characters. Each viewpoint (medical, legal, religious, and personal) was presented and then argued with dignity, respect, and complexity.

The series frequently takes this approach to complicated issues. I know of no news program that comes remotely close to this episode, in analyzing a complex topic so fairly and effectively. When so-called news programs today present a discussion about a complex issue like abortion, they typically have their own pro-life or pro-choice agenda. They select emotional experts who express extreme and rigid viewpoints, fail to define key terms, and encourage disagreement and distorted arguments. In short, they do everything they can to make the people who disagree with them look foolish.

Another *Law & Order* episode I watched with great interest illustrated why I feel the way I do about some defense attorneys. Titled, "DR 1-102," it originally aired in January 2002. In this episode, one of the prosecutors (Serena Southerlyn) is present at a hostage situation. She agrees to enter a store as a lawyer and meet with a male hostage taker to help negotiate the release of the hostage. But she doesn't tell him she's actually a lawyer with the district attorney's office. The hostage situation is resolved with no harm to the hostage or hostage taker.

However, because Southerlyn did not accurately identify herself as a prosecutor, she is considered to have deceived the man and violated an ethics rule (Rule DR 1-102). She now faces disbarment proceedings. This episode offers typical *Law & Order* complexity and balance. But, at the end, I still said to myself, "You have got to be kidding! Lawyers cannot engage in deception?"

I quickly went online and found the New York Lawyer's Code of Professional Responsibility. Sure enough, under DR (Disciplinary Rule) 1-102 Misconduct, it actually states "A lawyer or law firm shall not engage in conduct involving dishonesty, fraud, deceit, or misrepresentation." I didn't go to law school and the specific types of misconduct set forth in this rule might have some specialized meaning or interpretation. But by any normal reading of this rule, how can a lawyer defend an obviously guilty person in a criminal case? Simply claiming your guilty client is not guilty is dishonest and a misrepresentation. Apparently, the legal profession has created its own rules for what constitutes dishonesty and deceit.

Taking the question of deception one step further, I once testified as an expert education witness for the prosecution. It was a criminal case involving the sexual victimization of an adolescent child. As part of my testimony I told the jury that one of the reasons child victims sometimes lie about the nature and scope of their victimization is because they are ashamed and embarrassed about their compliant behavior. During cross-examination, the defense raised an important concern. He asked me how the jury could distinguish between a lie told by a child accuser who was an ashamed victim and a lie told by a child accuser who was not a victim and was making a false allegation.

What an excellent point! I certainly wasn't suggesting that any child or witness should be automatically believed, or that we should ignore a past history of lying. My answer was that the jury should listen to *all* the evidence, evaluate it, consider its consistency, and based on all those factors, decide whether a witness is credible.

I was recommending that the jury consider the totality of reliable and probative evidence. But the defense convinced the judge to prevent the jury from hearing some of it and then, knowing otherwise, had the nerve to argue the victim's allegations were untruthful and false. I did not learn of this until after I finished testifying. That's when the prosecutor told me the defense attorney had successfully filed motions to suppress evidence that would have given the jury a clear understanding of the sexual relationship between the offender and the victim.

So-called good defense attorneys do this all the time. Most shocking is the fact that defense attorneys (and the legal profession in general) view this type of dishonest behavior as ethical and admirable. The profession has developed a sophisticated, scholarly, and self-serving belief system to justify it – by arguing it's all part of providing a zealous defense for their clients.

I certainly have no problem with attorneys defending people who are innocent, or whose innocence is in doubt. I also understand the legal distinction between not guilty and innocent. Plus, "having done it" is not the same as being legally guilty. I'm not talking about insanity and diminished capacity defenses here. I'm not talking about attorneys helping a guilty client get the best deal. Most cases don't even go to trial. I am talking about attorneys using their skills and knowledge of the law to help guilty clients get away with crimes they factually, intentionally, and deliberately committed. It would obviously be equally wrong, if not worse, for prosecutors to prosecute someone they know with certainty is factually innocent, but they rarely try to rationalize such false prosecution as a good thing.

You can always argue that people are innocent until proven guilty. However, the fact of the matter is, defense attorneys often know that their clients are factually guilty. Some defense attorneys seem to deal with this by simply never specifically asking their clients if they committed the crime in question. Or they blindly accept their clients' lies – no matter how incredible, absurd, or unlikely they are. Defense attorneys know their clients lie to them all the time. They try not to concern themselves with a matter like factual guilt. A defense attorney once told me that he was under tremendous pressure in a case because he believed it was one of the rare times when his client was factually innocent. He said it was no big deal if his defense failed and a guilty man was convicted, but an innocent man's conviction would distress him.

With a factually guilty client, lawyers will plead their client as *not guilty*, file motions to suppress reliable evidence, try to impeach truthful witnesses, offer alternative theories of the crime with little or no evidence, and use mutually exclusive defenses (their client did not commit the crime, but if he did he was mentally ill). Defense attorneys have successfully argued to suppress evidence (videos, audiotapes, photographs) that unequivocally proves guilt – and then aggressively tried to discredit the child victim during cross-examination. Such tactics may be legal but they are also morally reprehensible and wrong. How can attorneys do all this without engaging in dishonesty, fraud, deceit, or misrepresentation – the very thing New York Rule DR 1-102 forbids attorneys to do?

I believe I know the answer in many cases. My experience with child molesters taught me that individuals, especially the more intelligent ones, can always find ways to validate bad behavior as being good. Lawyers are so absurd in their validation that they proudly claim something so obviously dishonest is actually noble, and that making the system work by using deceit and distortion to help someone get away with crimes should be admired. They are so ardent in their validation that they have institutionalized this idea, and teach it in prestigious law schools. And they are so audacious in their validation that they accuse people who disagree as being ignorant or unintelligent. Lawyers have been so effective in these efforts that the concept is usually praised and rarely challenged.

More than alternative facts, they have created an alternative universe.

In my personal experience, these efforts are magnified many times over in death penalty cases. Almost anything can be justified as part of efforts to prevent or stop the death penalty. For instance, in one capital murder trial, the defense attorney correctly asked a jury while reaching its verdict, to follow principles of objective fact-finding similar to the ones I set forth here. But he then proceeded to violate almost every one of them during his closing argument. Consistent with the unprofessional characteristics described in Chapter Five, he distorted the facts of the case including inconsistent use of definitions; claimed to have some special knowledge of how the crime was committed; appealed to the emotions of the jury and attacked the messenger in the form of the individual investigators and experts who testified; alleged conspiracy theories about the prosecution; and engaged in self-deception by accusing the prosecution of doing exactly what he was doing and filing a motion for mistrial over improper comments by the prosecutors in their closing. These arguments may influence many people, but they also reduce the chances of reaching an objective, and correct, decision.

In another capital murder case I testified in, the defendant abducted, sexually assaulted, and murdered a six-year-old girl. His first death penalty conviction was overturned on appeal. For the retrial, DNA evidence was able to positively link him to the crime scene. His defense at the second trial consisted primarily of an alternative theory of the crime – the victim's grandfather had killed her. The defense attorney had no real evidence of this. Yet he was allowed to force the grandfather to testify, claimed he fit some alleged profile, and introduced his past criminal convictions; all things the attorney could not have done if the grandfather had been the actual defendant in the case. The grandfather, dying of cancer, had his reputation dragged through the mud.

And yet no doubt that defense attorney and his colleagues were proud of their defense. While trying to prevent the death penalty, he provided his guilty client with a zealous defense. Who cares if it was dishonest? Ultimately, the jury again convicted his client. The attorney did not fight a second death penalty sentence because his fees for the next appeal would continue to be paid from a special capital litigation fund.

What troubles me is that such irresponsible tactics are not condemned and punished by the legal profession. They are praised and rewarded. I'm fully aware of much of the validation for what defense attorneys do to help factually guilty people to get away with their crimes: it is the rule of law, not man; truth and morality can be in conflict with the law; they are making the system work; they are holding the prosecution to a burden of proof; they are protecting the civil rights of the innocent; better that ten guilty go free than one innocent be convicted; everyone deserves a vigorous defense; the meaning of guilt is complex; and people complain about defense attorneys until they need one. In my opinion, none of this justifies such conduct.

When I was in the FBI, I couldn't officially work for the defense in criminal cases. I was a salaried FBI employee and as such, couldn't have any outside employment. I did, however, often talk with defense attorneys. I shared my knowledge and opinions. I sent my published materials about how to objectively evaluate cases to them.

I consulted on cases in which I told investigators or prosecutors that the totality of evidence did not support a guilty verdict. My material and comments on satanic ritual abuse certainly cast doubt on the guilt of many accused offenders in those cases. I've stated in my publications, "if the guilty are to be successfully prosecuted, if the innocent are to be exonerated, and if the victims are to be protected and treated, better methods to evaluate and explain allegations must be developed or identified."

After I retired from the FBI, I was free to officially work for defense attorneys. In the last seventeen years, I have been contacted numerous times by defense attorneys for accused child molesters.

They ask if I'm willing to work for the defense in such cases. Since I believe that innocent people are sometimes falsely accused of molesting children, I will help with the defense in those cases.

But before agreeing to do so, I told each of those lawyers *my* conditions for assisting in the guilt and innocence phase of such a case: 1) I must be convinced that their client is factually innocent, that they did not commit the alleged acts; 2) I only want to hear about things such as improper searches, poor forensic interviews, failure to give Miranda warnings, or sloppy police investigations if they indicate their client is factually innocent; and 3) If and when my evaluation of the total facts indicates to **me** that their client is factually guilty, my involvement in the case is over.

I realize some people might disagree, but they are *my* conditions. I understand that in this country individuals don't have to prove they are innocent. The burden of proof is on the prosecution. I cannot, however, help someone get away with sexually victimizing children when the evidence, as I objectively and expertly evaluate it, clearly indicates guilt.

Afterwards, most of those lawyers told me that wasn't a problem because their client was, in fact, innocent. However, I never again heard from any of those lawyers. As a result, I have not yet worked for the defense in the guilt or innocence phase of a criminal case. I have testified for the defense in the post-conviction or sentencing phase of cases, after guilt was determined. I have continued to furnish general information and my opinions to defense attorneys.

In my experience, *some* defense attorneys simply don't care if they help child molesters get away with their crimes as long as they get paid. Most of them, however, probably truly believe they are doing something important and worthwhile. They might even believe it's an honor and a privilege to defend guilty people. In either case, those attorneys seem to have no problem trying to legally exclude reliable, probative evidence that proves guilt beyond any doubt.

I disagree with that.

Their primary interest is not to search for the truth. Defense attorneys are not bound by the truth. Their primary interest is in whatever helps their client in an adversarial system of justice. Throwing mud on the wall and seeing what sticks is an acceptable strategy. In my opinion, their *need to believe* that they are doing a good thing by helping guilty criminals get away with their crimes is often influenced by ego, politics, power, and money. I am sure many defense attorneys would argue that my opinions about their efforts are influenced by my need to narrowly focus on the small picture of holding guilty criminals accountable for their behavior and not the big picture of the law and the U.S. Constitution.

By the way, in that *Law & Order* "DR 1-102" episode, the prosecutor who committed an error of omission by misleading the hostage taker and saving the hostage's life was privately reprimanded after the proceedings. She wasn't disbarred. Her fellow prosecutor, the character Jack McCoy, tells the disciplinary committee, "This was a unique situation where the assistant district attorney put her life on the line to protect us. When it was over, everyone walked out alive. This lawyer had a moment to choose between being a lawyer and being a person. What would we have all thought if she'd made a different choice?"

The elected District Attorney, character Nora Lewin, then replies to Southerlyn's thanks, "And I appreciate what you did, but if you wanted to save people, you should've become a doctor."

Yes, it's just a television program, but I have seen these dynamics at play in real life. The *Law & Order* website says that this episode is often used in law schools as a teaching tool for discussions on attorney ethics. I, for one, am offended if lawyers try to imply that standing up for that code of responsibility in a situation like the one portrayed on the TV show makes them somehow commendable. Especially, not when they daily commit deceit and misrepresentation in defending clients they know with certainty are guilty.

I hope that in their law school discussions students come to the conclusion that the code was misapplied in this fictional case. That it should be applied to those who use "dishonesty, deceit, or misrepresentation" to help acquit the obviously guilty.

Pointing out real flaws in the quality of evidence is right and honest. Inventing and misrepresenting flaws in the evidence is wrong and dishonest. There need to be more limits on what defense attorneys can do to defend *factually guilty* clients. What kind of professional ethics call good things "bad" and bad things "good?"

Although I have carefully thought about and considered for a long time the controversial opinions I expressed, I will admit they may be influenced by my own emotional and powerful need – punishment for bad behavior and reward for good behavior. I hate to see people, such as guilty criminals, get away with, and be rewarded for, bad behavior.

I enjoy seeing people who do the obvious but difficult, and right thing get rewarded. A case in point: one of my favorite movies is *Cinderella Man*, the true story of Depression-era boxer James J. Braddock. In the movie he is faithful to his wife, devoted to his children, overcomes poverty with honest, hard work, and winds up the upset heavyweight champion of the world.

I suspect my need is rooted in the way I was raised, schooled in a religion that taught me that salvation is earned by good deeds. My parents also taught me values, the concept of right and wrong, and a sense of responsibility. They taught it – and they lived it. I am still working hard on being more patient and forgiving.

CHAPTER NINE

"Truth Waits for Eyes Unclouded by Longing"
(Chinese Proverb, 6th Century BC)

Any book about evaluating information requires some discussion of mental illness and mental disorders. The most common misconception Americans have about mental illness or disorders involves confusion over the diagnostic differences between Psychotics and Psychopaths. Laypeople and the media constantly confuse and interchange the terms *psychotic* and *psychopath*. Occasionally they also throw in *psycho* or *sociopath* to make it worse.

People who have a psychosis are said to be *psychotic*. Schizophrenia is an example of a mental illness that causes psychosis. By definition, people who are psychotic have hallucinations, delusions, and disordered thinking, or a combination thereof. Hallucinations are sensory experiences, such as hearing voices or sounds or seeing things that are not there. Delusions are false beliefs, such as believing that one is being persecuted, loved by a movie star, or tracked by the CIA. Mental illnesses involving psychosis sometimes reduce a person's responsibility for a crime – such as with court findings of "insanity," "diminished capacity," or "guilty but mentally ill."

A *psychopath* is a whole different ball game; it is an example of a mental disorder. To avoid further complicating these terms, I summarize and simplify this concept as much as possible. The specific term *psychopath* has moved in and out of favor over the years. Today it's generally considered a type of personality disorder (a combination of the features of *antisocial personality disorder* and *narcissistic personality disorder*). It isn't something you have; it's what you are. It is a description of a cluster of personality characteristics. Many view the condition along a *Psychopathy* continuum. In 1982, Psychiatrist Richard M. Restak wrote an excellent book about this type of personality. Its title *The Self Seekers: Understanding Manipulators, the Predominant Personalities of Our Age*, conveys much about the book's premise.

It's often said that psychopaths have no conscience. This is not accurate. They do have a conscience, but it does not conform to the consensus of society's standards. They have a disregard for community standards of behavior. Psychopaths set their own standards. They can rationalize and justify almost anything. Since their behavior usually doesn't violate *their* conscience, however, they experience little or no feelings of guilt or shame. They are usually only sorry they got caught. Psychopathic types tend to be impulsive and have difficulty delaying gratification. The past and future matter little. They focus primarily on the present. They don't like to consider accountability for their behavior.

In the early days of the FBI BSU, the instructors developed a mnemonic device to help students understand the characteristics and nature of psychopaths. They used the word C-H-A-M-E-L-E-O-N; a lizard that changes appearance in different environments. The C stood for Cunning; the H for Habitual Criminal; the A for Actor; the M for Macho; the E for Egotistical; the L for Low Frustration Tolerance; the E for Experimenter; the O for Operator; and the N for No Guilt. Psychopaths often lie just because they enjoy manipulating others. When confronted with their lies, they go on the attack – the best defense is a good offense.

With criminal justice issues, we often focus on psychopaths from lower socioeconomic groups who are violent criminals. We forget about the better-educated ones who are successful businessmen, politicians, lawyers, and Wall Street brokers but who are also crooks and frauds. I am fully aware there are individuals who deliberately manipulate information and intentionally lie simply to achieve their goals. Like Professor Harold Hill in *The Music Man*, this psychopath might create unreasonable fear and concern, convince you he has a solution, and then sell it to you to make money or gain power. But these psychopaths are not universally condemned, especially by those who believe their objectives are worthwhile. The end justifies the means.

I realize that some of the people who hyped and exaggerated satanic ritual abuse as well as the number of missing children, fall into the category of psychopathic con artists. But in a weird way you could understand and almost admire their skill, focus, and planning. They had an objective, put together a plan, and implemented it, but not for the right reasons.

I also came to believe, however, that many people who responded to such emotional issues believed what they were saying was accurate. They didn't seem to deliberately lie. Without any corroboration and with so much evidence to the contrary, how could so many intelligent, well-educated professionals believe something – such as SRA – was happening? As I explained and repeated earlier, asking that question helped me realize that adults *tend to believe what they want or need to believe.*

To illustrate, a prosecutor who was building a criminal case against some therapists who were regularly treating adult survivors of satanic ritual abuse once contacted me. The therapists were collecting payments from their patients' health insurance. As a result, the prosecutor planned to charge the therapists and their accountant with medical fraud. He wanted me to testify that there was no evidence that satanic ritual abuse even existed. I told him what I knew about the lack of evidence supporting such allegations. I also said I didn't think my testimony would help his case very much. That's because in such a *criminal* fraud case he would have to prove that the defendants knew such abuse had not occurred, and filed the claims anyway. I explained that if, during cross-examination, I was asked to give my opinion about whether most therapists dealing with ritual child abuse actually believed it was happening, I would have to respond that I thought they did.

So, how could the prosecutor prove beyond a reasonable doubt that those defendants knew their claims were false? He then asked me how anyone could possibly believe something was happening if there was no evidence to support it.

"You have got to be kidding!" I replied. "People sincerely believe things all the time without real factual evidence."

Then I cited several examples, including two famous ones. Many Americans believe the assassinations of President Kennedy and Martin Luther King were due to elaborate government conspiracies – even though there is no real evidence to substantiate either belief. I reminded him that people tend to believe what they need to believe and selectively accumulate or discard evidence to support their beliefs. I never testified.

In that case and others, I struggled with how to word and precisely express what I had profoundly recognized about human behavior. I wanted to communicate that intellect and education had nothing to do with it. Smart educated people seemed just as vulnerable as slow uneducated people. Nor was this about common sense and real evidence.

I learned it was almost impossible to change such people's minds with logical arguments. They always had answers that maintained their belief system. The key to this tendency seemed to be the underlying needs or agendas. The stronger they were, the more resilient the tendency was.

Finally, I carefully crafted the precise statement I have repeatedly used here: "*Regardless of intelligence and education and often despite common sense and evidence to the contrary, adults tend to believe what they want or need to believe – the greater the need, the greater the tendency.*"

I was so proud of myself. For a brief moment I had delusions of grandeur, thinking I had discovered some new insight into the human condition. But as I continued my research, my bubble was quickly burst. I soon realized that scientific researchers were well aware of and documented this dynamic a long time ago.

Social psychologists call it *confirmation bias*. Nonprofessionals identify it with expressions like, "There is no such thing as an atheist in a fox hole" or "One man's terrorist is another man's freedom fighter." The first because, when confronted with death, you suddenly need to believe in God. The second because, in deciding who is a terrorist, your subjective situation plays a role. Back in my neighborhood in the Bronx, no one fighting for Catholics in Northern Ireland was considered a terrorist.

Then I learned that in 50 BC, Julius Caesar is quoted as having said, "Men in general are quick to believe that which they wish to be true." What I thought I had discovered was not remotely close to being recent. The final straw came when I discovered a Chinese Proverb from the 6th century BC, *"Truth waits for eyes unclouded by longing."*

I had discovered nothing. All I was left with were some examples, observations, and experiences about how this dynamic affects opinions and conclusions, including those in my own professional and personal life. I was generally aware of this concept but didn't really appreciate or understand its significance until I experienced it professionally and personally, and it directly affected me.

I now knew that many learned people down through history had recognized and written about this aspect of human behavior. To help me better understand it, I identified and read several current books on the topic (*see* Appendix II). In any case, I decided to add to the discourse about our need to believe by presenting my views and experiences from a plainspoken, law enforcement perspective.

I was intrigued by the fact that even some of the learned individuals who studied and wrote about it didn't seem to realize that as they formulated some of their observations, they (and I?) were doing the same thing. This is what I previously discussed as self-deception. They cite every example of exaggeration and bias by others, but then ignore and deny that they did the same in their study. No doubt many people would argue that what I say about defense attorneys in the prior chapter is an example of me doing the same thing. And I fully recognize and try to monitor this possibility in myself. Many other people, however, seem incapable of doing so.

We are always objective and right. *They* are always devious and wrong.

For almost everyone, confirmation bias can be a major obstacle to arriving at valid and fact-based conclusions. We would all like to believe that professionals can and do rise above such bias, but sadly this is often not the case. For example, consider the self-described "progressive" Democrat running for governor in Virginia in 2017. In his political ads, he called President Trump a "narcissistic maniac," then said we have to keep Trump's "hate" out of Virginia. He seemingly does not include his expressed hate for the President or recognize the irony in his statements. Apparently, this gubernatorial candidate does not recognize the irony in his own words – or the hatred he himself expressed for the President.

I've yet to identify the root source of people's underlying and varying needs to believe. Why do certain balding men believe that a comb over hairstyle will conceal baldness and make them look better? They must see something different than we do when they look in the mirror. As a bald man, I know about this from first-hand experience.

Why was my mother sure that professional wrestling was fixed; yet believed that roller derby was real? Why do certain people waste time or money on horoscopes, fortunetellers, and psychics? A Hollywood celebrity once contacted me and asked if I knew the name of a good professional psychic. To me the words *professional* and *psychic* taken together is an oxymoron. Why do certain elderly people need to believe things were so much better when they were young than they are now? Many of them share sentimental stories and photos of "the old days," via the chain emails I receive everyday. Why do certain people blame the government or a bank for their financial failures? They act as if no one told them they eventually have to repay their loans and what they charge on their credit cards. Why are certain people so quick to believe the worst about those they dislike and the best about those they like? Why do some people think they know everything and don't even need to consider other opinions or sources of information?

Why are certain people more susceptible to these needs than others? Why does it happen with some issues and not others? Edward R. Murrow is quoted as having said, "People believe they are thinking when they are merely rearranging their prejudices."

In 1993, a female writer for a national magazine interviewed me for a story about satanic ritual abuse. The article focused on one woman's story of being an adult survivor. I told the writer that I couldn't comment about a specific case without knowing all the details and facts. I could only comment on the phenomenon in general based on the many cases I had consulted on. She agreed, so we did the interview for the article she wrote.

When the article was published, that writer explored whether society and I would have been so quick to repudiate such accounts if thousands of men were offering them instead of women. She said she remained deeply troubled by the skepticism when so many of those women seemed credible to her.

I had tried, with minimal success, to clarify some misunderstandings about my interview comments when I was contacted before publication by the magazine's fact-checker. I did not base my conclusions on imprecise subjective judgments or a gender bias. I knew from my experience with SRA allegations that just because someone describes his or her victimization with strong emotion and sensory detail doesn't make it more credible, accurate, or true. In addition, I have a mother, three sisters, a wife, and a daughter. In the majority of sexual abuse cases I consulted on, the victims were female. I would never dismiss an allegation simply because it came from a girl or woman.

Years later this writer was interviewed about her newest book. From her comments and the views she expressed, it was clear to **me** she was an intense feminist. I considered the possibility that the issue with the 1993 article wasn't so much that I had dismissed the allegations because they came from women, but that she had been inclined to believe them because they came from women. I don't think I was the one who was influenced by a gender bias.

Interestingly, another female writer I met also had a gender-based perspective on these cases. She said one reason she became skeptical about allegations of satanic ritual abuse, particularly in the daycare cases, was because so many of the alleged offenders were female. In the McMartin Preschool case, all but one of the accused offenders were women. She felt it was literally a modern day witch hunt, designed to deflect attention away from men as the primary perpetrators of sexual victimization of children.

Recognizing that these abuse cases involved a dynamic significantly different from well-documented abuse cases was a valid reason to be skeptical. Her rationale was certainly a better reason to be more skeptical than the victims' *seeming* credibility was to be less so.

People with health problems often become highly vulnerable to con artists, quacks, and charlatans offering treatment or a cure. They can somehow believe that guy online has a cure for cancer but the government or drug companies are keeping it a secret. The placebo effect of medication and treatment is also a powerful example of the capacity of the need to believe. The elderly and people with financial problems become especially vulnerable to moneymaking con schemes. I knew from my many white-collar crime investigations while in the FBI that the primary reason too-good-to-be-true con schemes work is not because the offender made it so believable. No, it's because the victim wanted so badly to believe it.

Bernie Madoff operated a massive Ponzi scheme by convincing smart people that he could consistently give them exceptionally high returns on their investments with no risk. When it collapsed, few of them accepted any of the blame. What makes people vulnerable to such scams is not a lack of intelligence and education, but a want or need to get easy or unexpected wealth. The reason these victims are often embarrassed to report their victimization isn't because they were so gullible, but because they were so needy or greedy. Some people on the brink of financial ruin conveniently blame the government rather than their own bad decisions. They demand their money back, as if their greed is irrelevant.

Religion and faith seem to be another significant focus of some people's need to believe. Most people are in one of two religions (or absence of religion) – either the one they were born into that still meets their needs or the one they switched to when their religion of birth didn't. For people who cannot or prefer not to follow external rules, it's easier to just say you are spiritual, but not religious. I noticed that some Catholics rejected their religion about the same time their daughter needed an abortion, their son announced he was gay, or they wanted a divorce. I am not a religious scholar, but from what I have read and learned, in the sixteenth century, Martin Luther was a devout Catholic Augustinian priest. This is the same religious order that taught me in high school. However, Martin Luther struggled to live up to the high code of behavior in which he religiously and fervently believed.

Eventually he led a protestant reformation that taught salvation is not earned by good works, but received only as a result of faith and grace. My own mother shared this belief with many Protestants. Was Luther's new belief the result of objective study, divine revelation, or possibly a personal need? He also believed that individuals, not just the Catholic Church, should be allowed to interpret the Bible – apparently as long as their interpretation agreed with his. There are religions still around today founded on the belief that the world was going to end 150 years ago. The factual basis for the religion changes, but the belief in the religion does not.

The need to believe seems rooted in some combination of factors, such as financial situation, age, mortality, morality, personality characteristics, psychiatric disorders, and life experiences. It seems almost a version of the old debate about whether human behavior is determined by nature (genes, chromosomes, hormones), nurture (environment, upbringing, stress) or some combination of both. I quickly realized this was beyond my expertise. I did observe some common factors that were frequently involved (money, ego, self-esteem, health, paranoia, attention, money, politics, vulnerability, emotion, and religion), but I gave up trying to determine exactly where these needs come from.

So I began looking inward. Why was I apparently less vulnerable to this, at least in my area of professional expertise? I was heavily invested in the issue of sexual victimization of children. I tended to believe the children. In the first edition of *Child Molesters: A Behavioral Analysis* published in 1986, I actually stated that after interviewing a child victim, the investigator "knows what happened and now he must prove it."

In trying to understand what needs or wants influence the evaluation of information, I considered why when I evaluated cases of child sexual victimization I was generally able to maintain more objectivity as a professional fact-finder. I met and became aware of many individuals who were nonconformists – people who frequently challenged authority and conventional wisdom. I clearly was not one of them. Why was I able to process the same information in a different way? When dealing with such an emotional topic, why was I able to maximize the professional perspective, while minimizing the political and personal perspective? I came to the conclusion that the two biggest factors are: 1) how I came to my job and expertise and 2) my basic background and personality.

Over the years I've been asked many, many times how I came to specialize in cases involving the sexual victimization of children. Strangely enough, I often wished I could simply offer some emotional story involving my personal victimization, the victimization of a close family member, a calling from God, or an extraordinary decision to dedicate my life to helping innocent children.

However, you now know the real, and rather simple, answer: "Because I wanted to get married." One thing in my life led to another, and for somewhat practical and selfish reasons I chose to specialize in crimes against children. That is the main reason I spend time telling the story of my journey. My work was rewarding, important, and fulfilling, but I was not drawn to it for some sentimental or altruistic reasons. I was just an FBI agent doing my job.

In addition, the FBI paid me the same salary every two weeks. It was not dependent on how many children were abused or abducted. If there were no more abused children, I would have been assigned to other work. And it certainly made no difference to me financially in which direction the evidence led. By the time I retired from the FBI, my late-in-life expenses were also over. I had paid for my two children to go to college, and for my daughter's wedding. I had always lived within my means, had no credit card debt, and had stayed married to the same woman.

When I retired from the FBI and decided to become an independent consultant, my wife asked me what would happen if no one hired me. I told her we would continue to live the way we had for the last thirty years. We would have a nice home, drive a nice car, and take a few nice vacations. There would be no mansion on the lake, no BMW, and no around-the-world cruises. Nonetheless, it turned out that as a private consultant in the area of crimes against children, I earned more money than I ever dreamed. However, Kathy and I lived primarily on my FBI pension. I didn't want to be influenced by a need to maintain some new enhanced standard of living. As a consultant, I wanted to be free to turn down cases and render opinions based on an objective evaluation of the facts. I worked for both plaintiff and defendant attorneys in civil cases and frequently gave them opinions they didn't want to hear, which limited my billable hours.

My background and personality also are significant factors in my perspectives. I was a well-trained and experienced investigator for ten years before I ever came to the BSU. I was more skeptical and to some degree had adopted a law enforcement type bias of assuming most people are lying unless you know otherwise. My work experience had also desensitized me to many aspects of these cases. Plus, my threshold of bizarre was different than that of most people. I had learned to use the defense mechanism of intellectualization to shield myself from the details. Effective use of this mechanism helps people to emphasize thinking, while minimizing feelings. It allowed me to be less personally offended or emotional about deviant sexual behavior and the related graphic details.

There was no such thing as too much information for me – the more the better. This was made a little easier by the fact that in my consulting work with the BSU, I was usually one step removed from some of the worst aspects of these cases. Reading reports and looking at photographs of horrible crimes is not as difficult as actually interviewing the victimized children or being at the crime scenes.

During my many years of teaching about sex crimes, I learned something interesting about people's reactions. When it comes to sex, Americans seem to love to joke about it; look at images of it; and use dirty words, metaphors, or analogies to discuss it. But many have a difficult time simply talking about it in plain English. This is especially true when discussing behavior motivated by bizarre sexual paraphilias, such as urination, defecation, or bondage. Even when I wasn't trying to be funny, some people attending my presentations would respond with almost a nervous giggle. Many attendees, usually a mix of men and women, were unaccustomed to someone openly discussing sexual behavior in plain words, as nonchalantly as if talking about the weather.

When my son Ricky was about ten years old I was with him in a bookstore. As I was looking at professional books, I thought he was looking at children's books. Suddenly he came over to me and asked me to explain a joke in a book he was reading. When I asked him the name of the book, he responded *Truly Tasteless Jokes*. I told him that wasn't a book for children. He said the book was funny but one joke did not make any sense. The joke? "Why can't Dr. Pepper have any children?" The punch line? "Because he comes in a bottle." My son said that Dr. Pepper coming in a bottle was not funny and asked me if I could explain it. I didn't know where to begin. So I changed the subject and repeatedly avoided answering the question in the time following this incident. Several years later, my son came to me with a big smile on his face and simply said, "I know." Because I had taken the avoidance route used by many parents, I now did not know exactly what he knew.

To make a point, I have told this story many times during training classes. When I get to the joke punch line, some people laugh because they think it's funny, some people don't laugh because they don't think it's funny. But many people don't laugh because they, like my son, don't get it either. However, no one has ever raised their hand and asked me to explain the joke. They might wait until the class is over or ask a very, very trusted friend. I learned that people are reluctant to ask questions about sex, or to admit they don't know or understand words or terms related to sex. Because I was in the business of communication, I made it a practice to talk clearly and bluntly about sexual behavior in my professional presentations. Of course, depending on the audience, I would make some variations. Some readers here may even feel I have been too explicit or graphic in discussing sexual topics.

Broadcasters often give viewers advance warning about graphic details in an upcoming story. After viewing the story, I usually have a hard time determining what the so-called graphic details even were. A few years ago, I awoke one morning and Kathy told me she had to turn the television off because some killer was describing in graphic details the crimes he had committed. She said it was horrible. I learned it was a broadcast of the *BTK killer* allocuting his crimes at his sentencing. Later in the day I watched, as it was re-broadcast. What my wife had thought was horrible and shocking, I thought was a light overview of his crimes.

He didn't mention the kind of details I dealt with everyday in my work. Of course, I keep reminding myself that most people cannot deal with such information. Not being shocked or surprised by it makes it easier to maintain objectivity. It doesn't mean you remain untouched by the consequences to victims. Like a surgeon or mortician, you have to learn to do your job in a professional way. Jim Reese was a fellow BSU member; he was the Unit's expert in stress management. He once told me "you have to build walls to protect yourself – just don't forget to leave a few doors."

Using the three-legged-stool approach (training, research, and case consultation) while doing my job also provided the balance and perspective I could not have achieved otherwise. Doing research and training gave me a break from case consultations, and reinforced the importance of objectivity and the need to define and consistently use terms. They helped me to apply these skills to my case consultation work. Also, because I used this approach to focus in one area more than thirty-five years, I have developed an extensive knowledge of it. Due to my long-term and extensive work in this one specific area, I came to know more about more aspects of the sexual victimization of children than almost anyone. This has been both a blessing and a curse.

It's great to know far more than most people do about a specific topic, but it makes it frustrating to hear others discuss the topic with a lack of insight and in-depth understanding and with an over-abundance of emotion. As an example, I used to enjoy watching *The O'Reilly Factor* on Fox News. Because we come from similar backgrounds (middle-class, Irish, Catholic educated, and from the New York metropolitan area), I could relate to O'Reilly's traditional values. He certainly could become pompous with guests, but I tended to agree with many of his views. He often said what I wanted or needed to believe.

However, when O'Reilly discussed sexual victimization of children, I tended to disagree with many of his emotional and simplistic views. Here my need to believe was superseded by my own extensive knowledge about one topic. I recognized when he didn't consistently define and use terms, misrepresented the literature and research, appealed to emotion, and oversimplified and generalized from anecdotal examples. Was this spin in the no spin zone or did he sincerely believe what he said? I then wondered if he might be doing the same thing with other topics. If so, I realized I might not recognize it because I lack the expertise, desire, or time to overcome my need to continue to believe what I wanted to believe.

For example, one of O'Reilly's favorite topics was the passage of Jessica's Law in all fifty states. It was part of his efforts to protect the "urchins." That issue, however, wasn't as simple as he made it sound. Currently approximately forty-four states have passed the law in some form or another. In my opinion, many of those states passed it because of emotional and political expediency rather than how effective it was.

The law was named for a child victim who was abducted and murdered. As mentioned, most child molesters **do not** abduct their victims and ninety percent of offenders who do abduct their victims **do not** kill them. On the map O'Reilly has on his website, the states that passed the law were shown in purple, said to have been Jessica's favorite color. The law's provisions vary but typically they address mandatory sentencing and long-term probation and monitoring.

What many people don't realize is that its provisions often apply only to cases with children under the age of twelve and only for certain sex offenses. Case examples cited to illustrate the need for its passage sometimes involve children and sex offenses not even covered by the law.

In addition, mandatory twenty-five-year prison sentences for first offenses, which the law often requires, can discourage plea-bargaining and limit prosecutor flexibility. Avoiding stressful trials is often extremely beneficial to child victims. Many people support lengthy prison sentences but few people want their taxes raised to pay for the high cost. Whatever anyone's opinions are about the law, any meaningful debate should include discussions of the exact version of the law being considered, the precise definitions of the types of cases to which it would apply, what it will and won't do, and the data to support its effectiveness. Objectivity should surpass emotion and politics.

Another reason I was able to keep my objectivity was because I didn't have any significant ego needs or wants. Sure, I enjoyed some recognition and status, but essentially I'm just a middle-class kid from the Bronx. My parents raised me to be humble. In spite of my boast about knowing so much about the topic, I still have a hard time responding when I am asked during testimony if I am an expert.

My parents also taught me to be responsible and to do the right thing. I realize some people might find my opinions offensive. But being right, or on the right side, is more important to me than being popular or famous, especially in my old age.

Former President Harry Truman is quoted as having said, "It is amazing what you can accomplish if you don't care who gets the credit." That seems to be a fading characteristic in today's world of reality television and people being "famous for being famous." Some people send tweets about what they had for breakfast. This level of narcissism, as seen on social media, is beyond my comprehension.

I also realized that I have a logical and orderly mind. I

tended to process information like an encyclopedia. I can name all the U.S. presidents in order. Not from pure memorization, but because I mentally cataloged the historical context in which each of them served. My brain is a trivia machine. Maybe this personality characteristic is one reason I was drawn to investigative work. At least in some areas, I seem to have the ability to objectively collect information, evaluate it, and attempt to corroborate it. But I also recognize I have personal needs and wants, and am vulnerable to their effects on my opinions. When evaluating information and making important decisions, I try to monitor this tendency in myself.

I tried to follow my own recommendation about considering the middle ground, when I thought about the debate concerning the celebration of Christmas in the United States. I recognize my potential Christian bias. It's common to complain that Christmas is becoming too commercial. This sentiment is even expressed in the holiday classic movie *Miracle on 34ᵗʰ Street*. But many people seem to forget or ignore this movie was made in 1947.

Christmas, as it is celebrated here in the U.S., has actually always had a strong commercial component. Some Christian religions even opposed its celebration. Christmas is a holiday that, as its name indicates, has a religious essence related to Christianity. Yet the government has made it a national holiday. Is this the establishment of religion and a violation of the First Amendment? Is it politically correct to say "Merry Christmas" or "Seasons Greetings?"

To me, there is reasonable middle ground. In the United States, the Christian holiday of Christmas has also become a culturally significant and widely shared secular holiday. Common elements of its celebration include Frosty the Snowman, Rudolph the Red-Nosed Reindeer, buying gifts, and even Santa Claus. Yet these all have little to do with the practice of religion. Because of the benefits of shared cultural experiences and a boost to the economy, the government should encourage its secular celebration by everyone without requiring its religious celebration by anyone. It makes sense to me. Some of the happiest days of my life were spent being Santa Claus to my two children as they grew up.

In recent years, I have become increasingly pessimistic about the direction the country is heading. I actually hope it's part of the previously mentioned need of old people to believe the country was great when they were growing up but is now in decline. It appears to me, however, that fewer people even care about objectivity and facts, and more people make decisions based on emotion and political correctness. Many believe they are right and don't care what anyone else thinks. They defer to no experts or outside authority. They are adherents to the old adage – "I have my mind made up, don't confuse me with the facts." They are happy with their uninformed opinions.

Carl Sagan, in his 1996 book, *The Demon-Haunted World*, said it well:

"I have a foreboding of an America in my children's or grandchildren's time – when the United States is a service and information economy; when nearly all the manufacturing industries have slipped away to other countries; when awesome technological powers are in the hands of a very few, and no one representing the public interest can even grasp the issues; when the people have lost the ability to set their own agendas or knowledgeably question those in authority; when, clutching our crystals and nervously consulting our horoscopes, our critical faculties in decline, unable to distinguish between what feels good and what's true, we slide, almost without noticing, back into superstition and darkness. The dumbing down of America is most evident in the slow decay of substantive content in the enormously influential media, the 30 second sound bites (now down to 10 seconds or less), lowest common denominator programming, credulous presentations on pseudoscience and superstition, but especially a kind of celebration of ignorance." (*see* Appendix II)

In this same book, Sagan also references and quotes from two of my publications on the topic of satanic ritual abuse investigation to illustrate and support similar points he makes.

News and fake news, facts and alternative facts, science and pseudoscience, lies and truths – our society seems confused at best about what to believe and how to form opinions. Properly processing significant information becomes harder in a world filled with polarized politics, extreme social media rhetoric, and public authentication of responses based on emotion. Information now comes from ever expanding, harder-to-verify online sources.

I have some suggestions to help people moderate the effect of *the need to believe*. My hope is to influence people to think more about and better understand how they process information. This is crucial when making decisions about significant issues. I'd like to at least stir the pot a little, and shine a brief light on the value of critical thinking. In doing so, I'm following the advice of author Edward Everett Hale, who around 1902 is quoted as having said,

"I am only one, but I am one. I cannot do everything, but I can do something. And because I cannot do everything, I will not refuse to do the something I can."

CHAPTER TEN

"The Insidious Encroachment by Men of Zeal"

As I wrote this book, I became increasingly doubtful about my ability to change anything. I wondered if my suggestions were even realistic. People believing what they need or want to believe seemed to be an ingrained and basic human characteristic. Every day I read, saw, or heard narratives where the media, politicians, and others would fail to define terms, inconsistently use definitions, misrepresent facts, and communicate using emotion-driven clichés. All of which further distort any discussion.

Advocates with anecdotal experiences based only on their own situations were repeatedly given precedence and status over specialists who objectively studied data or researched a problem for decades. I regularly watched as emotion and politics overwhelmed objective fact-finding.

It's like Louis Brandeis is quoted as having said, "The greatest dangers to liberty lurk in the *insidious encroachment by men of zeal,* well meaning but without understanding."

This simultaneously discouraged me and invigorated me to try to make a difference in people's thinking. Could I influence just a few people to more objectively evaluate information when making important decisions? Other scholars have certainly tried to address this issue, but maybe the more down-to-earth, personal story of an FBI agent might resonate for some in a different way.

In any case, I have tried to identify and explain some of my lessons for life, which I learned during my professional search for facts. In compiling the suggestions here, I was forced to confront the same choices I made years ago when developing training programs. Do I present practical recommendations and suggestions likely to be implemented or do I present principles and ideals to strive for?

I decided to present primarily ideals, and let the reader decide what to consider and implement. As with my efforts to address the sexual victimization of children, I decided that my measure of success would simply be whether I made the situation better than it was before. These are the lessons I learned along my journey, as well as some basic suggestions for readers.

At the risk of sounding like a grumpy old man chasing kids off his lawn, I've included a few personal observations and comments to illustrate points; as well as my analysis of some relevant current events. I don't ask you, the reader, to blindly accept any of it. But please use the type of critical thinking I suggest when considering them. At the same time, I recognize that emotion can be a practical and important factor in making some decisions.

I know from experience that what I am proposing can be difficult and time-consuming to implement, as well as sometimes unpopular. Truthfully, I have no simple solutions for complex problems. Each person has to decide if any decisions they are considering are worth the effort. Many will just continue to engage in selective interpretation of information and believe what they want or need to believe.

Most people don't want to be told their beliefs are based more on personal needs than objective facts. Young adults, in particular, often defer to no one else's opinions, research, or expertise. The advice provided here is intended for the people who sincerely want to learn accurate facts and make better-informed decisions. It is not intended for those who think they already know or don't care about the facts, or who want to influence and manipulate others by intentionally misrepresenting or distorting these facts for their own agenda.

Kurt Andersen describes the absurdity of American individualism by saying, "If I think it's true, no matter why or how I think it's true, then it's true, and nobody can tell me otherwise."

To give some perspective, I'll describe an interaction my wife and I had some time ago. For some reason, Kathy became preoccupied with the JonBenet Ramsey murder that occurred in Boulder, Colorado. She read every book and article she could find and watched almost every television program about the case. I never shared with her what I knew from the detailed consultations concerning this case that I had been officially involved with – both inside and outside the FBI. I will also not discuss them here because that information was provided to me in confidence and it remains a pending case.

I let Kathy do her own information gathering and merely listened as she explained her various theories and conclusions. If at some point she *mistakenly* came to the conclusion that JonBenet Ramsey had been murdered by aliens from outer space, it really didn't matter to anyone else. There were no serious consequences for whatever she came to believe or its basis.

Many decisions that we make have few major consequences. Often they aren't a choice between an absolute right and wrong. Instead, they are more a matter of making a reasonable decision at the time. It is hoped you consider any advantages and disadvantages so you don't later wind up smacking your forehead moaning, "Gee, I never thought of that."

The process I am describing and recommending here is less relevant to minor or inconsequential decisions. Sometimes, though, depending on the circumstances, you might want to improve your knowledge and increase the chances of making a better-informed decision. At the same time, remember that I'm certainly not trying to complicate life and turn each person into a junior G-man investigator.

We live in a world filled with what is referred to as *fake news* and *alternative facts*. Although definitions can vary, *fake news* is generally defined as media reporting that consists of deliberate misinformation or hoaxes disseminated with the intent to mislead for financial or political gain. The key word here is "deliberate." I would add to that definition by including **any** media report that is not accurate and balanced. The news then becomes inaccurate or false. By my definition, these inaccuracies don't have to be deliberately made.

Whether due to producers' and reporters' burdens, bungling, or bias, any inaccurate news story is essentially fake news.

Because the term was popularized targeting the Trump administration, *alternative facts* are generally harshly defined as basically a fancy term for deliberate lies that further your agenda. I would add to this definition *seemingly* conflicting information resulting from confusion over definitions and their inconsistent use.

It is more important to consider how opinions are formed and decisions are made when they involve important issues such as budget deficits, elections, police shootings, climate change, gun violence, and healthcare, as well as important medical and financial personal choices. In these situations, a modified version of the three-step process I repeatedly used in my work might at least be helpful.

Those steps are: 1) gather diverse information, 2) assess and evaluate it, and 3) attempt to corroborate or verify it. These are not always separate and distinct steps used in strict numerical order. They overlap and interact. And adaptations to the process need to be made depending on people's ability to access reliable and detailed information, subject matter expertise to evaluate it, and resources to corroborate it.

The first step is to *gather diverse information* from as many different sources as possible. Repeatedly ask yourself how you know what you think you know. Don't just listen to the sources or points of view you already agree with. If you are a fan of FOX News, occasionally watch MSNBC. Alternate between watching the national news on CBS, NBC, ABC, CNN, and PBS. If you like Internet blogs, read a newspaper. Diversify your use of social media. Talk to people from other backgrounds. In December 2017, the AP reported on the development of a browser extension that hopefully alerts users to fake and biased news stories and helps guide them to more balanced coverage. The plug-in, *Open Mind*, is intended to "help get people out of the habit of associating on social media only with people who share their viewpoints and reading biased news coverage skewed toward their beliefs." How well and objectively it will work remains to be seen.

Somebody once said that everyone is entitled to his or her own opinion, but everyone is not entitled to his or her own facts. So keep an open mind and consider all possibilities. Ask yourself if you or the source of your information might have an agenda or special interest. Sometimes it's hard to know. The more diverse your sources are, the less problematic individual biases are. Understand that information can be presented from personal, political, and professional perspectives, or some combination of all three. A personal/emotional perspective is less problematic if it does not masquerade as being a professional/objective one. Although I believe that information from the professional/objective perspective is the most valuable, it might be useful to deliberately gather information from all three perspectives – just know the difference.

For a long time I internally debated about which is more problematic: the person who knows what he or she is saying is wrong but deliberately says it anyway – or the person who sincerely believes what he or she is saying is right but it is not. Knowing full well it is untrue, for personal or political gain, some will deliberately play to their audience and tell them what they want to hear, often intentionally creating alternative facts or fake news. The person who deliberately lies is fully aware of what they are doing and makes a conscious decision to do it. Their reasons for doing so may be well intended or contemptible, but it is an intentional, well thought out process.

The person who misevaluates information and comes to sincere but invalid conclusions can be admired for at least not being deceitful. But such flawed thinking can often be more damaging and harder to change. In their first trial for murdering their parents, the Menendez brothers used the mitigating defense of "imperfect self-defense" to reduce their murder charge. It is defined as an honest but unreasonable belief that your life is in danger.

Is it worse for a gossip newspaper to know a story is inaccurate or fake news, but print it anyway? Or for a respected newspaper to print a story they incorrectly believe is accurate due to their biased or sloppy journalism? Do popular media commentators truly believe some of the unreasoned distortions they set forth every day? In my opinion, such inaccurate journalism may be due more to bias than malice – but it still constitutes fake news. I do not know the answer to this dilemma. It's hard to measure the proportional harm of each. But, depending on the significance, motivation, and consequences of the resulting conclusions, both approaches are potentially problematic. True professionals should rarely do either. Since the two are not mutually exclusive, however, some choose to do both.

I have repeatedly seen this dilemma with expert opinions offered in civil and criminal cases. Some experts will say almost anything they are asked to say – regardless of whether they truly believe it. Other experts can convince themselves to come to an opinion that conveniently helps their client while enabling them to be paid even more as an expert.

I've worked on civil lawsuits involving child sexual abuse and the Catholic Church. While doing so, I discovered that Church officials have a specific term to refer to the act of deliberately misleading people without technically lying. The Church argues it is justified to avoid scandal or protect the common good. It is known as the *Doctrine of Mental Reservation*. Some Church officials said that this was learned in the seminary and is individually determined by conscience. As another simple example, my wife (and many others) believes it is okay to tell "little white lies" to avoid hurting someone's feelings.

An important part of gathering diverse information is determining the definitions for the terms being used. According to legend, a Chinese Proverb says "The beginning of wisdom is to call things by their rightful name." Many people use their own, inconsistent definitions for their terms. Good researchers are usually among the few people who understand the importance of consistent, operational definitions. You can't accurately measure or count something without first specifically defining it. Media reporting of their research, sadly, often ignores or misrepresents those operational definitions and thus creates confusion and distortion in media reports.

Readers now know that I have become almost obsessed with the importance of definitions and their consistent use. This fixation is rooted in the three-legged-stool approach I used in my work that included research and training. In addition to determining the definitions of the key terms used, attempting to determine whether those definitions are consistently used is also important. Do not assume that your definitions of common terms are the same as the ones being used by others.

Specialized, new, or slang terms can become common without people knowing their precise or varying definitions. Just think about the social media definitions of familiar terms like *friend* and *like*. Most people don't know the subtle but important difference between similar terms such as *mental illness* and *mental disorder*, *psychotic* and *psychopath*, *rape* and *sexual assault*, *debt* and *deficit*, *overweight* and *obese*, *murder* and *homicide*, *republic* and *democracy* and *casualty* and *dead*. What exactly, constitutes *hacking* or *sexting*? Use a dictionary, urban dictionary, or computer to look up and even Google any terms, phrases, expressions, and variations you are unsure of. Then use those definitions properly and consistently.

During my career, I repeatedly saw how difficult and important it was to precisely and clearly define even seemingly basic but key terms like *sex* and *child*. Emotionally charged and inconsistently applied terms (*poverty, sick, casualties, homeless, missing, justice, abused, harassment, rape*) that lump together widely diverse and complex issues can create major problems when seeking solutions. As I learned with the term *missing children*, a vague, imprecise umbrella term is often of little value in trying to deal with the specific parts encompassed by it. Other than involving *children* who are somehow *missing*, the diverse and complex components (lost, injured, benign episode, runaway, family abducted, stranger abducted) have little in common. The broad umbrella term makes emotionally dramatizing the entire problem easier but makes realistically finding solutions for the distinct variations harder. Statistics that combine the number of individuals "wounded" with those "killed" and the number of homes "damaged" with those "destroyed" can make it hard to determine the true scope of a problem and find the best solutions.

This definition problem was succinctly summarized for me when I heard a debate moderator on CSPAN state that "Most of what passes for disagreement is just confusion." Blurred distinctions between *sexual misconduct, sexual harassment, sexual abuse,* and *sexual assault* can cause confusion about the nature of the specific underlying behaviors. Precisely what constitutes sexual misconduct or sexually inappropriate conduct? They are poorly defined, fill-in-the-blank terms for which those reading or hearing them just insert their own definitions for a wide range of behaviors. The definition of sexual harassment is also diverse. Sexual harassment is a bad thing. Sexual assault is a bad thing. They are just not the same thing. I know from experience that conflating the terms and blurring distinctions in behaviors can create problems. Sexually motivated exposure and fondling could be aspects of sexual harassment, but are primarily sexual crimes. What is the standard of proof for such allegations? What should happen to those who engage in such behavior – loss of reputation, employment, money, or freedom? Linking them all together along with child molestation through #MeToo Twitter posts increases short-term attention but has limitations for achieving workable long-term solutions. Eventually, overly broad and exaggerated generalizations are likely to result in unsubstantiated allegations and fuel a backlash that will damage the credibility of underlying valid issues.

What concerns me most, however, about #MeToo is the word "too." There are significant differences between what is being included under this hashtag. Some of those differences are important, especially for child victims. By definition, sexual harassment and sexual assault are unwanted. Child molestation is a serious crime whether wanted or not by the child. Many children, especially adolescents, are groomed rather than forced into sexual activity. As discussed, such compliant child victims often experience *say no, yell, and tell* guilt and inaccurately describe how they were victimized as a result of societal attitudes and prevention programs (and hashtags?) focusing only on *unwanted* sexual activity.

I would hate to see a victim pressured to misrepresent the nature of his or her child molestation, to feel part of a hashtag support group. It is my unqualified opinion, but repeated experience, that children who have to misrepresent the actual nature of their victimization to parents, friends, therapists, and investigators do not recover as well, and sometimes get worse, compared to those who don't. A prior inaccurate account of child sexual victimization might also make it more difficult to investigate and prosecute a case.

In my experience, the confusion created by calling different things by the same name and the same thing by different names is a significant cause of apparent, or alleged, alternative facts. Two different estimates concerning the number of missing children don't mean one estimate constitutes an alternative fact. The difference might be due to distinct but equally valid ways in which the concept of *missing* is defined. Again, this is why it's so important to determine the intended definition of key terms before coming to conclusions. Another part of the problem occurs when the media often has to tone down, change, or use vague terminology so it won't offend or shock their audience. The result just confuses them.

During the 1990s, a well-known author wrote an op-ed piece in the *New York Times* expressing his belief that convicted child molesters should all be sentenced to life imprisonment, but not the death penalty. Someone from the Diane Rehm Show, which airs on NPR, contacted me. They wanted to do a radio program on this piece with the author, a mental health professional, and me. Each of us would share our diverse perspectives on the opinions expressed in the article. I thought this would be interesting, so I agreed to do it, and travelled to the radio studio in Washington, DC.

As the program began, the op-ed author quickly clarified that he didn't believe that all child molesters should be sentenced to life imprisonment – only those who were psychopathic, sadistic, and predatory. At that point, the mental health professional and I agreed with him. Once the author had precisely defined his terminology, whatever differing opinions had existed among the three of us disappeared. It was like an episode of *Saturday Night Live* where

Emily Litella (Gilda Radner's character) is corrected over her editorial confusion about a term, only to then say, "Never mind." Now what would we do for the rest of the program? It was spent primarily discussing how to determine which child molesters are psychopathic, sadistic, and predatory.

In ancient Greece, Themistocles deliberately lied to Athenian citizens to force them to prepare for war against the Persians. As a result, they eventually defeated the Persian invasion in the 5th century B.C. and saved Athens. Many politicians and activists are advocates of the expression, "Never let a serious crisis go to waste." They often have no problem deliberately misrepresenting the facts of an incident (Vince Foster suicide, the Tawana Brawley case, or the Ferguson, Missouri police shooting) to further their agenda. They call this spinning the story for their purposes. When politicians today suddenly change their positions or opinions, they usually explain that they have conveniently evolved. If true, this is a good thing. However, I remain skeptical.

Politicians, however, often play definition games. During my work in the mid-1980s with the Attorney General's Commission on Pornography, I saw how the difficulty in getting a consensus definition for the term *pornography* was an obstacle to meaningful discussions and coming to objective conclusions. Political agendas interfered with agreeing to joint definitions.

As I was specifically asked to do, during my testimony at the opening hearing, I showed the members of the Commission the full spectrum of images, from nudity to extreme sexual sadism, possibly considered pornographic. As I showed the images, I would repeatedly and sincerely ask, "Is this pornography?" In a 1986 book titled *United States of America vs. Sex*, Penthouse International ridiculed me as "the bald G-Man" famous in law enforcement circles for his eye-opening "Overview of Pornography" slide show. The fact is I had never done this specific presentation before or since. They apparently doubted the sincerity of my question and the complexity of my point by mockingly stating, "'Is this pornography?' agent Lanning asked the panel with a straight face." I was, however, totally serious and sincere – and making an important point.

Pornography is another one of those fill-in-the-blank terms that are rarely clearly defined. The term *adult pornography* actually has little legal meaning. For many it could be defined as sexual explicit material just beyond what they like to view. It is often confused with the legal term *obscenity*.

The term *child pornography*, however, does have legal meaning, but with slightly varying legal definitions. Determining that an image is child pornography is not as easy as people think. Even investigators sometimes don't understand the precise legal difference between simple nudity – innocent family photographs, works of art, medical images – and what the law commonly refers to as the lascivious exhibition of the genitals. I have been involved in several criminal and civil cases in which photo developing/printing or computer repair companies have reported such questionable images to law enforcement for investigation. The fact that investigators personally find the images offensive or wouldn't ever take such photos of their own children is legally irrelevant. The proper legal evaluation of questionable images often is based not on the visual depiction alone, but on the total context of how the images were produced, obtained, saved, or used. Because a significant portion of the population takes innocent family photographs of their children naked, lay people need to be generally aware of the legal definition of child pornography.

The scandal involving former President Clinton is the epitome of political definitions on steroids. President Clinton deliberately confused people by relying on alternative, narrow, or specialized definitions of terms like "sexual relations" and "is." Politicians like to refer to this as the "parsing" of words and they are usually good at it. That is fine, as long as the listener understands what is happening.

The recently renewed federal law, commonly called VAWA – Violence Against Women Act, is actually gender neutral. The first person prosecuted under it in the 1990s was a woman whom I believe had her husband killed. In pointing this out, Democratic Senator Leahy recently was quoted as saying, "A victim is a victim, is a victim." If that is true and the law is gender neutral, why is it called the "Violence Against Women Act?" From my experience, the answer is politics! That's how you play on emotions, get a law passed, and get votes. When the Republicans balked at some changes to the renewal of the act, they were attacked for being anti-women not being anti-victim.

Around 2006, a legal publication reporter I'll call "Clark" contacted me. Clark asked me about a quote attributed to the U.S. Attorney General, and said that during a recent speech, the Attorney General said, "At any given time, 50,000 predators are online prowling for children." Clark told me he had contacted the Attorney General's office and verified the accuracy of the quote. When Clark asked them for the source of that statistic, they said they would get back to him. So he then contacted the Child Exploitation and Obscenity Section (CEOS) at the U.S. Department of Justice, the FBI, and the National Center for Missing & Exploited Children (NCMEC). Staffers from all three agencies told him they couldn't confirm that number. The Attorney General's Office finally called Clark back, and advised that the statistic had come from the NBC *Dateline* program "To Catch a Predator." Obviously, it was his staff, and not the Attorney General himself, who identified the statistic and wrote the speech.

Clark said he then contacted NBC *Dateline* to get their source, and was told the statistic came from someone in law enforcement, whose identity they could no longer remember. However, "they had also confirmed it with Ken Lanning, a retired FBI agent and expert on these matters," Clark said.

That's why Clark was calling me. He asked how I arrived at the number. I said, "I hadn't." I told him that I had, in fact, been interviewed for the premiere episode of NBC *Dateline's* "To Catch a Predator." But, that interview took place **before** I learned they were covertly communicating with, and then meeting, offenders. Had I known they were conducting their own investigations using non-law-enforcement civilians, I would never have agreed to do the interview.

In any case, I told Clark that if *Dateline* had asked me about such a number, I might have responded that it was possible – but I was not the source of the number. I told him that I tended not to use specific unknowable numbers like that, for a wide variety of reasons. What is a predator? What is online? What exactly is prowling? Only in the United States? During what time frame? How do you count something you cannot define?

Clark then asked if I had any idea where the number came from. I told him that was a very intriguing question. I explained that over my many years of dealing with crimes against children that specific number had been brought up before. In the early 1980s during the hysteria over pedophiles and missing children, the number abducted each year was most often cited as 50,000. By the late 1980s, during the hysteria over satanic ritual abuse of children and Satanists sacrificing children, the number murdered each year was most often cited as 50,000.

"It seems like when we don't know for sure how large a perceived serious crime problem is, we default to 50,000," I said.

"But why the number 50,000?" Clark asked.

"I don't know for sure," I said, "but it's like a Goldilocks number – not too big to be ridiculous, but not too small to be ignored. It's also a nice round number."

I was partially joking, and Clark kind of laughed, but he included my Goldilocks comment in his full article. National Public Radio (NPR) later interviewed me about my entire interaction with Clark and his article. Because the NPR interview has been rebroadcast numerous times on NPR stations all over the county, many people heard it and have asked me about it. For some reason, it is the Goldilocks comment they remember most.

But the important point of this story is not "Goldilocks" or the number 50,000. The takeaway is: Why did the staff of the U.S. Attorney General use NBC *Dateline* as his source for a quoted crime statistic? The Attorney General and his Department of Justice are the main source of most reliable national crime statistics. It seems like all NBC *Dateline* needed to do in order to become the **credible** source of a crime statistic cited by the A.G., was to provide a number the A.G.'s office liked. If NBC *Dateline* had said there were only three online sexual predators and investigators were wasting tax dollars investigating the cases, they would have been viewed as fools or as having a politically motivated agenda. Instead, *Dateline* was quoted because they told the Attorney General's office what they wanted or needed to believe.

At the risk of being labeled racist or homophobic, and using two very sensitive and complex topics as examples, I'd like to briefly discuss how some of my recommendations might be applied. The first is police shootings of black males. The second is access to gender designated public facilities. Both are divisive issues, and I believe that clearer definitions would add to better understanding. This would also help to unite us, rather than pull us apart. I know many will disagree and claim my approach is simplistic and naive.

Obviously, I have no easy answers, especially to the broader issues involved. But I'd like to believe that instead of offering emotional anecdotes designed to appeal to passion rather than reason, or calling people names, we would do better to analyze reliable and consistently defined research, which might lead to a far more open and honest discussion. This would surely be for the benefit of everyone affected by either issue.

Considering history, the extremely emotional response to *police shootings* of African Americans is perfectly understandable. Instead of rioting and arguing over whose lives matter, however, I think an increased, objective study and analysis of the known cases could benefit us – as well as help find some solutions to the shootings.

It's important to be distinct and precise, when trying to find such answers. For instance, the significance of important distinctions can be lost when lumping incidents together under one label. As I previously pointed out, a vague, imprecise umbrella term is often of little value in trying to effectively deal with the specific parts encompassed by it.

Applying this process, the one I use myself, a researcher would need to gather, evaluate, and corroborate pertinent and accurate data about the details and variations of cases. *The Washington Post* now maintains a "Fatal Force Database" of such cases. Although all databases and statistics have limitations, this one indicates that the number of blacks killed by police has decreased every year since 2015 and 16 of the 233 blacks killed in 2016 were unarmed. This analysis might include behaviors by the police and the victims, which worsened or improved the situation. It could also include verification as to whether an epidemic of the specific cases exists. This might be a problem that cannot be completely measured by numbers alone, but research could help us recognize that different *types* of shootings need different *approaches.*

For instance, police can legally stop someone based on race and appearance if a suspect's appearance fits a known description. A specific police shooting might be justified. Sad to say, when studies have been done, many people respond by attacking and silencing the researchers instead of critiquing the methodology and the findings. As with missing children, once the true nature of a problem is determined and understood, it's harder to exploit the perception of the problem for some other agendas. More detailed and reliable research concerning these incidents needs to be done. In a speech at Howard University on October 25, 2017, former FBI Director Comey is quoted by *The Washington Post* as stating, "It's ridiculous and frightening that in the United States of America in 2017 we don't know how many people were shot by police last week, last month, last year."

But, as I discovered with SRA allegations, the more emotional the issue, the less likely it is that even good, objective research will be considered – much less accepted. Maybe the underlying cause of this problem is racism, but providing insight into the dynamics of specific incidents, and frontline strategies to defuse it, might help save lives now as we continue discussing the larger social justice issues and identifying long-term solutions.

I have known about individuals who are transgendered for decades. And I've professionally studied the issues surrounding them since the early 1980s. Thirty-five years ago, it was believed that knowledge of this condition could be a valuable part of an informed investigation of certain sex crimes. Back then, a transgendered person was considered to be an adult who believed he or she was not his or her apparent birth gender, was under the care of a doctor and therapist, and was in some stage of gender reassignment surgery. Today, being transgendered can be established simply by a subjective claim rather than an objective standard, gender reassignment surgery is considered private or irrelevant, and the condition is being identified in young and prepubescent children. There was an excellent Frontline program on PBS called *Growing Up Trans* that discusses some more recent insights into and the complexity of this issue. Hormone therapy for transgender children – either to delay puberty in the undesired gender or increase it in the desired gender – is a recent, controversial practice. There are not many studies on the long-term effects of such therapy.

I empathize with individuals who truly are transgendered. To influence public opinion, however, the emotional debate over access to traditional gender restricted rest rooms, locker rooms, or fitting rooms has been presented as either "You can no longer discriminate against bullied transgendered children" or "There can no longer be separate and private facilities designated for men and women." How the issue is presented can influence the public response. It is rarely pointed out that for purposes of many recommended nondiscrimination policies, being transgendered can be based simply on an individual's subjective feeling and claim at a given time. Dressing as or appearing to be your preferred gender is actually irrelevant.

If such policies had been in place back in 1955, any female simply by *claiming* to be a transgendered male on a specific day would have had the right to enter the pool area at the public high school where dozens of boys and I were swimming naked. Many would argue that no one would claim to be transgendered if they weren't. That's because they are not aware of the lengths to which many need-driven sex offenders will go to satisfy their sexual fantasies and urges. I am. This does not even consider the sexual curiosity of typical adolescent children. For those who doubt my insight, just consider some of the diverse, high-risk, compulsive, and eccentric sexual behavior allegedly being engaged in by all those accused of sexual misconduct.

Some assert there is a war against women, while supporting those who believe that gender is fluid, or that a woman is simply anyone who claims to be a woman. The most basic distinction in humans is being denied, while discrimination based on that distinction is being asserted.

Again, I have no simple answers but emotion-based ranting and name-calling does little to reasonably address the topic without creating new and more problems. Polarizing emotion dominates the discourse (discrimination/hate vs. privacy/enabling sexual predators). Solutions cannot ignore the right to privacy and long-held social norms and customs *justifiably* based on the sexual attractions of the vast majority of the population. We need calm, objective analysis and dialog. In this debate, maybe the biggest impediment is the lack of clear and consistent definitions. There must be an independent and objective definition and determination of who is transgendered. Reasonable accommodations can be worked out as they have been for years.

Another difficulty today in understanding definitions is that advocates and the media often talk using politically correct clichés and expressions. People making emotional arguments to convince others tend to oversimplify, exaggerate, and often have a short-term, idealistic view of history. They will make statements like "Children are not supposed to die before their parent" and "This is the first generation of children that will not be better off than their parent." It is amazing how often such statements are blindly accepted and applauded as the discussion moves forward. They sound like they are true, but they are often not. Throughout history, most parents had children die before them. To wind up with a few adult children, you had to have many births. Queen Anne of England was pregnant eighteen times. None of her children lived to adulthood and all died before her. It could be argued that the Protestant Reformation in England took place in part because three of the sons of the first wife of Henry VIII died in infancy. Abraham Lincoln had four sons. Only two outlived him and only one reached adulthood. My mother and my wife's father and mother all had siblings die in childhood. In exploring my family tree, I learned my paternal grandmother was one of ten children, three of whom died before their parents. Although these are obviously only anecdotal examples, with a wide variety of infectious diseases, no antibiotics, and difficult births, childhood death was common not too long ago in this country and still is in many parts of the world. In addition, throughout thousands of years of human history, most children were lucky to do about as well economically as their parents.

Other commonly used clichés focus on the meaning of living in a democracy. Do we live in a democracy or a republic? Do most people even know the difference? People seem to support democracy, the will of the people, and majority rule until their side or candidate loses. Then they focus on ignorant or apathetic voters and the civil rights that cannot be taken away by the majority. When public opinion changes, then the significance of majority rule and democracy changes. The Democrats supported the Electoral College system as set forth in the Constitution to elect the President when they thought it would guarantee the election of Hillary Clinton. When she lost, it quickly became undemocratic because the winner did not get the most popular votes. The definition of the winner was changed. Once again, inconsistent use of terms and ignorance of history fuel the divisions in our society. At least define the terms before the discourse begins.

I recently saw a video in which a cultural diversity instructor trying to make the point that the Mexicans crossing the U.S. border in the Southwest are actually *not* illegal immigrants because this land was once part of Mexico until the United States took it after the Mexican American War. This emotional argument sounds noble except that it ignores the reality of history. Mexico gained control of the Southwest prior to 1848 by taking it from Spain. Spain had gained control of this land by taking it from Native American tribes. Each of those tribes had gained control of the land by taking it from the tribe that was there before them. The Lakota Sioux didn't take control of their sacred Black Hills until around 1775 when they drove out the tribes who had been there before them. The Aztecs built a huge empire in pre-Columbian Mexico by physically conquering other native tribes. Some of those defeated tribes then helped Spain take the land from the Aztecs. That is the way the world has worked for at least 5,000 years. Similar time-based arguments are made about who has rightful claim to The Falklands, Jerusalem, Israel, and Palestine. Does all land rightfully belong only to the first group of humans who set foot on it? Who decides at what date conquest no longer matters? When I was a kid and we didn't want someone to play with us, we called, "gates closed." Did someone call "gates closed" in 1848? Do the wishes or votes of current inhabitants matter?

The point here is not a history lesson, but to recognize that with our short-term memories, biases, and our need to believe, we often assume the accuracy of statements as we talk in simplistic and emotional clichés that sound true but aren't. We need to be careful about coming to significant conclusions based on them.

One of the biggest emotional needs today seems to be the need to be or appear to be politically correct. It is like Hans Christian Andersen's fairytale of the *Emperor's New Clothes*. Many fear being seen as "unfit for their positions, stupid, or incompetent" so they speak in politically correct, emotion-driven clichés that are inconsistent with or ignore the facts. People, especially media commentators, often say what they are supposed to say without objectively evaluating the facts. Sometimes, someone has to engage in critical thinking and have the courage to say, "But he isn't wearing anything at all!"

Because of my expertise concerning the sexual victimization of children, I have noticed that idealistic discussions about *prejudice, tolerance, acceptance, inclusion, discrimination, bullying,* and *judgment* are rarely applied to disliked individuals such as child molesters. A television program is done on bullying, and it is stated that we should not harass, demean, or ostracize individuals because they are different. They emphasize things like the need to be inclusive and diverse, accepting of people in all their variations, and not being judgmental of people because you disagree with them or their behavior. Of course exactly what constitutes bullying is rarely precisely and consistently defined.

A few days later the same show does a program on child molesters. It is now okay to call them names ("predators") and ridicule, harass, restrict, and register them. This response seems to involve many of the same behaviors that were labeled as bullying on the prior program. I am certainly not equating bullying in schools or cyber-bullying with child molesting. But the inconsistent message seems to be that bullying itself is not intrinsically wrong. I guess that makes it okay to bully child molesters.

Maybe the test should be this: Does the judgment standard apply to child molesters, Nazis, and others you dislike? Is it acceptable to be judgmental of bad behavior? Is it acceptable to be intolerant of intolerance? For many, it now appears hate is acceptable to fight hate. Whether bullying is condoned or condemned seems to depend on who is being bullied and why. Those who bully online are often referred to as trolls. For many, bullying President Trump has become a badge of honor. Does bullying ever serve a positive social purpose such as helping to conform human behavior to beneficial norms? The attitude for many seems to be that only "unjustified" bullying against those they like and feel empathy for is bad. Anti-bullying zealots ironically often recommend bullying the bullies! This obviously involves subjective judgments and definitions. It is hard to avoid behavior such as *body shaming* and *micro aggressions* when their definitions are inexact or subjective. What I find even more amazing is that hardly anyone seems to recognize or admit these inconsistencies in their definitions, attitudes, and discussions.

Leakers are also often praised or condemned depending on what they leaked and why. For many, Daniel Ellsberg was a patriot for leaking the classified *Pentagon Papers* during the Vietnam War; FBI Assistant Director Mark Felt, as "Deep Throat," was a hero for leaking information from restricted FBI files during the Watergate investigations; and Edward Snowden was a whistle-blower for leaking highly classified documents about U.S surveillance programs. All of them broke the law, but are excused by many who believe the information they leaked needed to be made known to the American public. CIA Director Pompeo recently said he thinks disclosure of America's secret intelligence is on the rise, fueled partly by the "worship" of leakers like Edward Snowden.

The Russians may have also done something illegal by hacking into the computers of the Democratic National Committee, but are condemned as destroyers of American democracy for leaking accurate versions of unclassified emails. The Democrats have never claimed the hacked emails were falsified or altered in any way. In October 2016, President Barack Obama even attacked then-candidate Trump for making "irresponsible" claims about a rigged election and invited him "to stop whining and go try to make his case to get votes." The Democrats and the media did not seem especially concerned about the Russian hacking activity until after Hillary Clinton unexpectedly lost the election. Unlike with Ellsberg, Felt, and Snowden, with the Russians most of the attention is focused not on any need for the public to know the information they leaked, but on who obtained it and how.

There are three important but separate issues to be considered: (1) the source of the information, (2) how it was obtained, and (3) is it accurate. To the best of my knowledge, over the years and in a variety of ways, the United States has interfered in the politics of foreign countries. As this is being written, it has not yet been proven whether anyone from the Trump administration coordinated with or colluded in criminal activity with the Russians. Would the reaction have been the same if the Russians had hacked the Republicans and leaked their unethical activity to help Clinton get elected? I would like to believe it would.

Senator Barry Goldwater is quoted as having said, "Extremism in defense of liberty is no vice and moderation in pursuit of justice is no virtue." The current sociopolitical climate seems to be breeding extremists at such an alarming rate that even normal discourse is simply becoming the discourse of extremism. Extremists are often reluctant to expose the inconsistencies and absurdity of some of their arguments. I recently read an AP story about a "group of more than 100 hooded protesters, with shields emblazoned with the words 'no hate' and waving a flag identifying themselves as anarchists" violently attacking a small group of peaceful free speech protesters. It appears the street mantra of my childhood has changed to, "If I think your names hurt me, I can break your bones with sticks and stones." In spite of the first amendment, words (micro aggressions?) are punished more harshly than the resulting violent behavior. Which side does this violent behavior help and which side does it hurt?

In my efforts to professionally and objectively evaluate cases, I long ago realized that extremists and zealots often cite information out of context and selectively quote only that portion of research that supports their view. They cannot resist using hearsay, rumor, gossip, myth, and legend. They generalize from a few cases to all cases and make the unusual and atypical seem common and typical. Any source of information that engages in such practices should be minimized or ignored. I admit, however, that sometimes extremists advocating for radical, unjustified change is necessary to achieve moderate, justified change.

While and after gathering diverse information, the second and a key step is to *assess and evaluate* it before forming opinions or acting on it. Gathering information and determining definitions as part of the first step would transition into this second step. A good way to assess and evaluate information is to gather it from multiple sources, compare it, and be generally skeptical. In an October 2017 story about Trump administration changes to birth control regulations, the AP quotes Alina Salganicoff, director of women's health policy at the nonpartisan Kaiser Family Foundation, as stating, "The interpretation is very selective in terms of the science that they use. It's always possible to find one study that validates your claim, but you have to look at the quality of the study and the totality of the research. You can make an argument that you don't agree because of your religious or moral objections, but that is a different discussion."

Possible differences in definitions of terms should be recognized and reconciled as part of the assessment step. Be suspicious of any information that describes any large group of individuals as being all noble or all unscrupulous. Be cautious of information from politicians, commentators, columnists, bloggers, and experts whose opinions on any issue can easily be predicted. Why are the governors and state attorneys general who sue the President over an executive order they claim is unconstitutional almost always members of the opposing political party? Shouldn't such complex legal issues be based more on the law than on emotion or your party affiliation? Sadly, this often seems to be similarly true in predicting the decisions of Supreme Court Justices based on their judicial philosophy without even knowing the legal intricacies of a case. Again, consider the influence of personal and political perspectives and whether different perspectives are being inappropriately blurred and confused. Frequent use of emotional and pejorative terminology often indicates biases and changing perspectives.

For whatever reason, many people are gullible and naively believe whatever they are told, especially if it is what they want or need to hear. Information should not be accepted as fact just because someone you like said it and it's consistent with what you want to believe. People often decide to believe with no real valid basis. They do not know how to properly and objectively evaluate claims. This includes reporters and other professionals who should know better. When working at the FBI, my observations, analyses, and conclusions concerning offender and victim patterns of behavior were not based only on self-reported information, but on objective evaluation of the totality of the most detailed, reliable, and corroborated information available.

People are not victims or innocent of alleged wrongdoing merely because they claim they are. Depending on the consequences for believing, nothing significant should be believed and acted upon merely because someone said it. I learned from my work with sexual victimization cases that accounts of multiple events, on multiple occasions, over an extended period of time are not necessarily all accurate or all inaccurate. Because one aspect of a story turns out to be accurate or inaccurate does not mean that every detail is accurate or inaccurate. I also learned that shared claims by multiple accusers do not necessarily mean each is valid or accurate. Unless assessment and evaluation indicate alternative explanations, however, consistent statements from multiple individuals concerning the same events would obviously carry increased weight. For many reasons, victims sometimes delay disclosure of their victimization. Claims must be evaluated in their totality, consistency, and context.

Hillary Clinton struggled with this during her 2016 Presidential candidacy. She equivocated when asked if her husband's accusers from another decade should be believed, too. She is quoted as saying, "I would say that everybody should be believed at first until they are disbelieved based on evidence." Her response may be politically expedient, but it seems to suggest people are guilty until proven innocent.

Believers often point out, "Why would they lie?" Individuals lie or furnish inaccurate information for a wide assortment of reasons – including some that are not so obvious. This could include the need for attention and forgiveness, imperfect memory, and a need to believe. As I learned so well from my experience with allegations of ritual abuse, people, including victims and witnesses, should not be automatically believed or disbelieved. During coverage of allegations of sexual misconduct, reporters often ask or shout at executives and officials, "Do you believe the accusers?" The politically expedient answer may be "Yes." But the correct answer is, "I do not know; I have not yet seen the results of a competent, thorough, independent, and objective investigation."

Decisions that have significant consequences should be based on the evaluation of reliable and consistent details. Depending on who makes the decision, the results for someone accused could vary from criminal or civil jeopardy to loss of employment, reputation, or awards. In coming to an important and informed decision, the details of an incident are often more important than simply whether some imprecisely defined incident, such as *sexual misconduct* or *sexting*, may have taken place. The old idiom that "the devil is in the details" applies to many such situations. All of this is complicated by the fact that many people do not want to hear or know the graphic details.

I'm part of the first generation to grow up watching the news on television. And I'm sure there have always been problems with the quality and accuracy of reporting. But in my opinion, the more varied and competitive the media becomes, the worse the problem is. I believe the news media in this country have increasingly gotten sloppy, biased, and unprofessional. If we include online sources in our definition of the media, it is even worse.

When I was younger, I had no idea if John Cameron Swayze, Douglas Edwards, Walter Cronkite, or Huntley and Brinkley were liberal or conservative. They were news anchors providing information. The only television journalist from this era that I can remember ever being criticized as being politically biased was Edward R. Murrow. I suppose, however, that newspaper moguls like William Randolph Hearst used their newspapers to promote their agendas. There is also a large but frequently unrecognized distinction between editorial comment and reporting the hard news. In my idealistic memory, television news was once a public service provided by the stations and networks and was paid for by the profits from other areas of their business. No doubt, there were personal biases and a desire to attract viewers, but they did not appear so blatant or dominant.

The media seems to be increasingly influenced by a need to fill time, maintain audience share, be politically correct, and present their perspective about how things should be. Some stories seem to be selected based on whether they fit or can be spun so they seem to fit a social or political agenda. They give you their opinion instead of providing information so you can form your own opinion. For example, in a November 20, 2017 AP story discussing his response to allegations about Alabama Senate candidate Roy Moore, reporter Hope Yen points out that Donald Trump "was caught on tape bragging about forcibly grabbing women without their consent." Although his statements were obviously inappropriate and offensive, on the tape heard by millions, Trump actually said, "And when you're a star, they let you do it, you can do anything." It appears he was not bragging about "forcibly grabbing women without their consent," but about being able to use his "star" status to influence or gain their consent. To avoid misleading readers and to allow them to make up their own minds, at the very least, a more accurate description of the tape's content should have been included in the story.

Many of the stories the media present are poorly researched and explained. This is most obvious to me when they do a story about sexual victimization of children. Based on my assessment and evaluation of the media I consume every day, its broad credibility is declining and true objective journalism is dying. Whether or not they recognize their bias, media agendas based on a need to believe something decrease their ability to properly evaluate information and increase the likelihood of errors in judgment. As I have repeatedly said, the greater the need, the greater the tendency. But I am willing to consider that some of my opinions of today's media may be influenced by old age.

One media practice that drives me crazy is called "tease journalism." This is where promotional spots for the evening news are played throughout the day. They say things like, "serious disease spreading rapidly," "new threat to the environment," "famous actor dies," or "do cell phones cause cancer?" followed by "tonight on the evening news."

If these stories were truly news, it should be required that some basic facts be furnished in the promotion followed by "additional details this evening." It is clear that the primary purpose here is not to inform or provide any useful information but simply to get viewers. No matter how much they hype it at the commercial break and how important it sounds, you know if the evening network news has slotted the story in the last half of the program it will be of little real significance.

I was recently watching the evening network national news when they repeatedly hyped an upcoming story about a small plane crash by showing a brief video clip. When they finally aired the story, the full clip showed an accident in which no one was seriously hurt and damage was minimal – all with little more detail than what was in the hype. Why did they cover such a story with the limited time they have to cover all the world and national news? The answer seemed to be, as it often is, simply because this is television and they had video. It is as if they are competing with or becoming YouTube. If it is a trending or viral video, it must be news.

This is all worsened by the fact that we now have a twenty-four-hour news cycle. In my childhood, the evening television news was on for fifteen minutes. Now they have an entire day to fill. There is often insufficient time to check out details. Accuracy is sacrificed for ratings. I believe that one of the main reasons people develop exaggerated fears (e.g., abducted children) about modern life is because of the twenty-four-hour news cycle, and its need to fill the day and hype any story for ratings. A weather segment is now included on the network national news almost every night. On the ABC *World News Tonight*, the weather forecasters are usually made to stand outside with the George Washington Bridge in the background. Frightening images are rarely revisited after the fear hype value dissipates.

In a peculiar way, the local weather reports and the Weather Channel are even worse at this tease and hype. Even the weather is now used to hype ratings. Who would have thought that the weather would be daily high-stress viewing? If there is not a tornado, hurricane, blizzard, or flood in your area, they will find one someplace else. All my life I heard the expression that "he was not smart enough to come in out of the rain." Why should I listen to and believe any weatherperson or news correspondent stupid enough to actually go out into a storm? In spite of their claims, I do not need to see a guy standing out in the rain to know it is raining. And this often occurs even after the government has ordered evacuations. Instead of leaving the place being evacuated, these reporters travel directly to that spot as if they have some divine and important right to be there. The reporters drive around or stand outside in the storm at the same time they warn the audience to comply with the governor's order to evacuate or not drive.

If they cannot find scary weather anywhere today, they speculate about the future with frightening programs like *It Could Happen Tomorrow*. I once heard a Weather Channel promotion for a new scare program called *Forecasting the End*. It is hard to even trust the weather report when you realize they might exaggerate it to get ratings. I just wish they would tell me when it going to rain instead of telling me they "cannot rule out a thirty percent chance of possible widely scattered showers or a wintry mix sometime today."

The line between entertainment and news is also being increasingly blurred. Viewers often mistake the undocumented speculation and opinions expressed on cable news commentary programs as statements of fact. News programs and stories are used to promote entertainment shows and vice versa. Most of the morning TV news shows have turned into a party atmosphere where everybody appears together, laughs at each other's jokes, talks over each other's comments, talks in unison, and go outside the studio so you cannot understand what they are saying over the screaming of the crowd. It is not the party format, however, that concerns me. It is the blurring of the line between news, commentary, and entertainment; the deficiency in meticulous fact checking; and the loss of journalistic integrity. On one broadcast I watched, one of the morning hosts actually emphasized that the next story was really true. Was this in contrast to others that were not?

For forty years when I did training, I often asked members of the audience about their experiences with the media. I would first ask, "Did you ever work on a case about which there was significant media reporting?" Depending on the makeup of the audience, anywhere from fifty percent to ninety percent of the audience would raise their hands. These were primarily investigators, prosecutors and other child abuse professionals. Next I would ask them to raise their hand if those media accounts were a hundred percent accurate. Although you could argue about the degree and significance of any inaccuracies, of the tens of thousands of people I have asked, only one person ever raised a hand. My follow-up inquires were really rhetorical questions about how often they then have accepted, cited, referenced, or used the information in another media story and what makes them think that the information in those stories is any more accurate and reliable than the information in the one about their case.

In my FBI work, I also came to realize that personal and emotional involvement could be a big impediment to evaluating claims accurately and reliably. As emotion goes up, reason goes down. This influence can be so powerful that I have come to prefer the terms accurate and inaccurate to truth and lie. Someone's emotional version or interpretation of events or issues can be inaccurate without necessarily being a lie (a deliberate attempt to deceive). We have increasingly become a society in which emotion, anecdotal examples, and self-serving politics almost always override objectivity, research, and professionalism in influencing decision-making. Issues affecting millions are decided by the emotion-filled anecdotal accounts of a few.

Almost everybody engages in some exaggeration when trying to convince others of their opinions. This can play a big role in how stories gradually becoming exaggerated. Be alert for stories and accounts of events that seem too good to be true. Instead of repeating something you read, see, or hear as if it were a fact, consider phrasing it as something a source alleges or claims. When watching a documentary program, my wife will sometimes mention what someone did. I point out that is what was alleged they did. Because passionate individuals make for compelling story telling, they are often the primary focus in media stories in which emotions override objective evaluation. They are, however, usually some of the least reliable sources of accurate information. Think about how self-interest plays out in today's politics and elections. Be cautious about coming to conclusions based on information from individuals personally and emotionally involved with the issue.

The accurate presentation of objective research is often boring. Emotional conflict and simplicity are more appealing. Over the years and often without realizing it, media producers and reporters have often asked me complex questions. I have discovered they usually want short, snappy sound bite answers and not detailed, complex explanations. As readers now know, I am incapable of that. I was once asked to come on a network television program to explain to the audience what the age of consent for sexual activity with children was. I asked the producer, "the age of consent for what, with whom?" A sixteen-year-old girl might be able to consent to sex with the guy down the street but not with her teacher and not if he took sexually explicit photographs. If a young adolescent girl legally married an adult, she could consent to sex. When I finished giving examples and explaining for over an hour how complicated the question actually was, they no longer wanted me on the program.

Better decision-making also applies to financial matters. Billionaire Warren Buffet once stated that the most important key to his financial success was being rational, rather than emotional in picking stocks and investing. In the late 1980s, the federal government switched to a new retirement system for its employees. As an employee of the FBI at the time, I had the option of switching to the new system or staying in the old one. Unsure of what to do, I asked many of my fellow FBI agents about their choices. Most of them said they were not switching. When I asked why, they typically said the government would never give you a better system and/or some agent they thought was financially astute was not switching. None of these seemed to me to be valid reasons for making such an important decision. I eventually did extensive research and discovered that for most employees it was best not to switch, but for a few it was better to switch. My situation was in the small group for whom it was better to switch and I did.

Financial decisions are one of the areas where decisions can be important and need to be based more on objective evaluation of information and less on emotional distortions. In October 2017, Richard Thaler of the University of Chicago Booth School of Business won the Nobel economics prize for documenting the way people's behavior doesn't conform to economic models that portray them as perfectly rational. The AP quotes him as saying, "We need to take full account of the fact that people are busy, they're absent-minded, they're lazy and that we should try to make things as easy for them as possible." If you have the time and interest, it might be useful to read a book or take a class in statistics and what statistics actually mean and how they can be misused.

To help you better understand this evaluation process, I would highly recommend the following movie, documentary, novel, and song.

The 2008 movie is *Doubt*. It is about things to which I can especially relate – a Catholic School in the Bronx, New York, in the early 1960s and a priest accused of inappropriate sexual behavior with an altar boy. It takes place when the Catholic Church was undergoing radical changes. There is conflict between a more traditional, strict nun and a more liberal, lenient parish priest. The nun is convinced he is guilty and aggressively pursues the priest. The priest strongly denies the allegations. His guilt is never determined with certainty, and the priest is eventually transferred. As the movie ends, the nun admits she has doubts and wonders if her religious differences with the priest influenced her decision-making. Anyone who sees this movie and concludes with certainty that the priest did or did not sexually victimize the boy is entitled to his or her opinion. However, such a conclusion is unjustified based on what was presented. I know because this is the type of analysis I have been doing for more than forty years. The author of the script has skillfully provided enough evidence to be suspicious of the priest but not enough to determine his guilt beyond a reasonable doubt. There is "doubt." Recognizing uncertainty is an important lesson in evaluating information.

The 2004 documentary is *Capturing the Friedmans*. It is available on DVD with a second disc containing additional case information. The documentary traces the true story of a sexual abuse case from Great Neck, Long Island, in the early 1990s. Unlike many such films and programs, this film does not spoon-feed the audience one perspective. It gives the many parties involved with the case an opportunity to present their views. Many of the subjects interviewed in the documentary were members of the police, the prosecution, or were prosecution witnesses. It also allowed members of the accused Friedman family and other defense advocates to present their perspectives. Some of the key issues addressed are not mutually exclusive. The film allows viewers to make up their own minds, with doubt and uncertainty as plausible conclusions. This film is a true documentary and not propaganda as is often the case.

The 1988 novel is *Foucault's Pendulum* by Umberto Eco. It is a meticulously researched fictional murder mystery set in a factual historical context. Because I love history and crime stories, I thoroughly enjoyed the book. However, this book, more than anything else I found, helped me to understand how different individuals could look at the same information and come to totally different and convincing conclusions about what it meant. It was my Rosetta stone for understanding allegations of satanic ritual abuse.

The 1971 song is *Imagine* by John Lennon. My favorite kind of music from my adolescence is Doo Wop. I was never a big fan of the Beatles. However, I always especially liked the recording *Imagine* by John Lennon after he left the Beatles. The melody of this song was calming and peaceful. When my grandson Max was a toddler, he would get tears in his eyes just listening to it. For a long time, however, I was almost embarrassed that I liked the recording because I thought the lyrics were saying something with which I strongly disagreed. I thought the words were anti-religion and anti-military. Over time, I began to listen to the words more carefully and more openly. I realized I was actually ignoring the key word in the title of the song – "Imagine." The song does not say there should be no religion, no heaven, or no possessions, but only that we should imagine it. Although the song can mean many things to many people, for me it is imagining living our lives and making decisions without being influenced by our personal agendas, needs, and biases. The lyrics say many of the same things I am trying to say in this book. For me, it is a song about limiting the influence of external agendas when making decisions. I recommend enjoying the song while carefully listening to the words.

The third and maybe most difficult step for the average person is to *verify or corroborate* the information gathered and assessed. Again, the three-step process I am suggesting often involves going back and forth between each of the steps with each one complementing and supplementing the others.

Most people don't have the time, skill, or resources to conduct an independent investigation or hire private detectives. In some instances, it might be best to wait until others with those resources, such as law enforcement and the criminal justice system, can determine the accuracy of criminal allegations. My prior suggestions concerning gathering information from diverse sources, objectively assessing and evaluating it, and considering it in totality may constitute a type of verification. This is made more difficult by the fact that there are individuals (lawyers, politicians, businessmen) who, for a variety of reasons, don't want people to know all the available accurate information. To influence opinions, they prevent access to it or misrepresent its content. Before it was passed, how could the average citizen come to an informed opinion about "Obamacare," when the politicians made it difficult, if not impossible, to learn what it entailed? Speaker Pelosi actually once said, "We have to pass the bill so that you can find out what is in it." In 2017, the same Democrats then criticized the Republican health care bill because they had not been told what is in it.

Particular caution and attention needs to be paid to all political and special interest ads. They are almost always filled with distortions and inconsistent definitions, misleading and inaccurate information, misinformation and propaganda, or flat out lies. How much difference does it make whether the misinformation comes from the Democrats, Republicans, the Russians, or someone else? Very often you cannot even tell who the true sponsor of the ad is. This is important in attempting to corroborate claims.

It is common for political campaigns to use law firms to hire the researchers to ensure that their opposition research is protected by attorney-client and work product privileges. The ads are often designed to appeal to people's needs and wants. No one should ever provide their vote, support, or money based on such ads. To whatever extent possible, all claims and accusations in these ads must be independently verified and corroborated before responding in any significant way. In September 2017, the Associated Press reported that two Democratic U.S. Senators would introduce legislation to enhance transparency for online political ads, requiring social media companies like Facebook and Twitter to keep a public file of election ads and communications and make reasonable efforts to ensure that election ads are not purchased directly or indirectly by a foreign national. Why limit it to online ads and those purchased by a foreign national? Concern over spreading disinformation should be applied to anyone doing it. All political ads to varying degrees constitute influencing, interfering with, meddling in, or fixing an election.

Any opportunity to independently verify important information or access original source material should be taken. The amount of corroboration necessary to take action based on information is dependent upon the consequences of such action. Listening to speeches, press conferences, and other original sources is better than listening to media accounts of them. It is especially important to try to verify the true source of information obtained from the Internet. Sources such as USAFacts, a website that organizes thirty years of data from more than seventy local, state, and federal government agencies into a centralized hub that will give people a clearer picture of how the government makes and spends money, might be useful in verifying information in some situations. There are websites available to check out the urban myth-type information often disseminated online to gullible people by individuals with political and personal special interests. A local newscast where I live has instituted a news segment called "Verify." So far I have only seen segments verifying relatively insignificant stories.

Many older people have a tendency to believe the country is falling apart and it is time to spread the alarm. They often forget to verify or corroborate alleged examples they are provided. Instead of checking them out, they just pass them on to friends and relatives in chain-letter-like emails. If such an example turns out to be exaggerated or inaccurate, their credibility and the credibility for their arguments are damaged. If you only want to reminisce, just enjoy them.

If a media story or email link mentions an article or study about something significant to you, consider first reading it in full and then checking its source. Sometimes it is almost impossible to determine the true source of phone calls, texts, tweets, comments, and other social media communications. Much social media communication appears to involve unsubstantiated speculation

or intentional misrepresentation by individuals with an agenda –
including the Russians. During the American election campaign
from 2015 to 2017, in addition to thousands of targeted online ads,
Russian backed accounts allegedly used 80,000 Facebook posts to
reach 29 million Americans. Then, through "likes" and "shares" by
"friends," reached 126 million Americans who did not know where the
posts originated. It is hard to know how much just seeing such posts
influenced the election. As suggested, nobody should be making his
or her voting decision based on such unverified online information.
However, some of the posts could have been accurate or no more
inaccurate than those coming from the American political parties and
Political Action Committees (PACs). Many seem more concerned
simply about the source, rather than the content or accuracy of the
information posted.

In the late stages of the 2016 presidential election, a story began
to spread on the Internet about a pizza restaurant in Washington,
DC, that was part of a large child sex trafficking ring linked to the
Democratic Party. It spread rapidly over many social media platforms.
The story has been labeled "Pizzagate" with allegations of symbols
related to satanism and pedophilia; "cheese pizza" being code for "child
pornography"; underground secret tunnels; and links to high-profile
child abductions. I was slightly flattered to be called by an individual
who had read my material online and was seeking my opinion about
the story. This was an easy one for me. It clearly appeared to be a
variation of the type of case discussed back in Chapter Four. Although
it should be objectively investigated, it had all the characteristics of an
urban legend designed to appeals to the dual needs of those wanting
to believe child molesters are part of an expanding evil conspiracy and
Democrats or the government are corrupt and destroying America.
Mainstream media aggressively tried to expose its absurdity, but many
still believed it, including an individual who called me and another one
who showed up at the restaurant with a gun. Why? It is most likely
because they wanted or needed to believe it.

When confronted with information beyond my expertise, I
always tried to find knowledgeable and objective experts. I also tried

to at least apply the principle of common sense. Does it sound reasonable? Does it fit within the template of probability? Does it make sense? Is it plausible? Is it consistent with documented similar situations? Is it consistent with my life experiences? Does it pass the smell test?

In October 2017, I received an email from a friend with a photograph showing some of the members of the Seattle Seahawks NFL team in their locker room. The coach and several players were slightly crouched and appeared to be laughing. A player in the front was holding an American flag that was on fire. A caption asked any viewer to note the laughing and suggested the photo should go nationwide to test the NFL response. Somehow I suspected this photo just did not make sense. It did not pass my smell test. As a behavior-focused person, I was immediately skeptical of the apparent laughing response of Pete Carroll, their sixty-six-year-old head coach, to such activity. I tried to verify the authenticity of the image by at least doing a quick Google search. I quickly found several references about this particular photo controversy. According to FactCheck.org and others, it appeared to be a hoax involving a photo first published in January 2016 by the Seahawks and then altered or Photo-shopped. Several references showed the original photo without the flag and pointed out flaws in the altered photo (e.g., no smoke, player's hand in the flames).

In a bizarre definitional fine point, some pointed out that this was not really *fake news*, but a *meme*. I did a little research on the concept of a meme (i.e., an idea, behavior, or style that spreads from person to person within a culture), but it seems to be a distinction beyond my comprehension at my advanced age. The bottom line is this flag burning did not happen. As long as that is understood, I will leave the symbolism to others. Did the left, the right, or the Russians originate this false or misleading story? Does it matter?

There is an old but basic principle commonly referred to as Ockham's razor, that recommends that simpler explanations are generally more reliable than complex ones. This principle does not constitute scientific proof but is a good guide for verifying claims.

Those making the claims bear the burden of proof. People shouldn't fall for easy explanations for complex problems because the rationale fits their agendas. For example, the 2011 shootings in Arizona involving U.S. Congresswoman Gabrielle Giffords or the 2017 shooting in Virginia involving U.S. Congressman Steve Scalise and Congressional aides have little to do with uncivil political discourse or gun control as it is used and argued by so many. Such shootings are almost always rooted in mental illness or disorders and the lack of resources and ability to identify and effectively treat them. Thus, these shooters are usually triggered by something few in the media want to discuss. Then, based on how the media cover these crimes, this practically guarantees the shooter will become famous. Proposed gun-control laws that follow rarely address the realities of the complex cases exploited in an attempt to pass them.

Once again, as I learned with many emotional issues, a vague, imprecise umbrella term is often of little value in trying to deal with the specific parts encompassed by it. To achieve their real agenda, the media and others will lump together the high-profile case with a wide diversity of unrelated cases (gang shootings, hate crimes, armed robberies, police shootings, stalking, suicide, accidental shootings, gay bashing, domestic violence) under a common link or label – such as *gun violence*. Some of the measures offered may be of some value in addressing some aspects of gun violence, but rarely do they **prevent** the types of crimes that politicians use, emotionally and politically, to get those laws passed.

Most of these mass killing cases, including some terrorist incidents, have two very important factors that are rarely discussed in any detail and proposed solutions seldom address. One is the difficulty in identifying, effectively treating, and involuntarily committing mentally ill individuals who are dangerous. This is primarily due to the high cost of maintaining such secure mental institutions. It's also due to legal decisions that limit the ability to institutionalize individuals against their will, unless they are proven to be a significant danger to themselves or society. Even when warning signs are identified, little can be done to them. If they are involuntarily committed, it is usually only for a brief period of time until they are no longer considered a danger.

The truth is, most people with mental illness are not violent. The main problem is the unpredictability of their violence. There is no simple solution to this conflict between the rights of an individual and the protection of society. Too many people who are a minimal risk would have to be confined to protect us from the few who are dangerous.

As Dr. Park Dietz first helped me recognize, the other key factor that proposed solutions rarely discuss or address is the significant role that media coverage of these offenders play, in ensuring that the notoriety and attention such killers typically seek is achieved. This is often the irrational motive that the media continue to pursue, but repeatedly ignore. The media and other so-called experts are quick to point the finger at other causes for such violence (e.g., gun control, media violence, video games, hate groups, alt-right, uncivil political discourse, bullying, mental illness, or President Trump), but don't want to address the role media reporting plays. By achieving the desired notoriety and attention ("deadliest mass shooting in U.S. history"), the next unbalanced killer is then increasingly motivated. Maybe the media would be less inclined to do this if they were required to make it more obvious by using the current popular sports term for such an individual – the G.O.A.T. (greatest of all time).

There is no rational motive for such irrational crimes. Going from an ignored or failing nobody to an infamous and widely discussed somebody may be as close as we can get. Of course, some of these killers are so emotionally and mentally disturbed, it is hard to make any sense out of why they do what they do. Such cases obviously need to be covered by the media. In my opinion, however, there should be voluntary standards and limits, not censorship, concerning how such offenders are portrayed and discussed.

There is one component of society that is in a good position to follow this third step of advice to verify and corroborate information – it is the mainstream news media. Their failures have caused me the greatest disappointment because I still get most of my news from television – local, network, and cable. They have the resources to check out and verify stories before they disseminate them. Similar to law enforcement, their work should be the product of objective fact finding. Analysis and exposing wrongdoing are good things as long as they are done fairly and objectively. Premature speculation based on incomplete and distorted information serves no worthwhile purpose, other than possibly an unjustified increase in ratings or circulation.

When I was researching Satanic Ritual Abuse cases, I wrestled with the concept of what makes a crime a satanic crime and how to verify it. Some told me it was the presence of Satanic symbols (e.g., upside down crosses, pentagrams) at the crime scene. For my research, I decided to define a satanic murder as one committed by two or more individuals who rationally plan the crime and whose primary motivation is to fulfill a prescribed and documented satanic ritual calling for the murder as set forth in verifiable records. Simply alleging, based on folklore (blond-haired, blued-eyed virgins; pregnant women on Christmas; body carving), that what occurred in a certain case comprises a prescribed and documented satanic ritual does not constitute verification. I am certainly not aware of every murder in America, but by this definition, I have been unable to identify even one documented satanic murder.

As part of BSU research, another agent and I interviewed a convicted serial killer named John Joubert. Due to strange symbols carved into the bodies of his victims, some of his killings were suspected as being Satanic. Some people believed it was a marijuana leaf, the French fleur-de-lis, the Boy Scout symbol, or a satanic pentagram. We asked Joubert and he laughed. He claimed it was not a symbol at all. He just slashed the body with diagonal, intersecting wounds until his anger subsided. Could he have been lying? Of course. But there was nothing in the records or our interview to indicate otherwise. He was executed on July 17, 1996.

This analysis over what makes a crime satanic is certainly relevant to today's controversy over whether we are dealing with terrorism or Islamic terrorism. When is it appropriate to blame or identify an ideology and not just individuals for violent behavior? Does the percentage of Islamic leaders and followers (thirty percent of a few billion is still millions) or the existence of well-documented and widely accepted Islamic religious texts (Quran, Hadith) seemingly supporting or condoning the violence matter? Objective analysis and corroboration, not politics, should provide the answer.

In summary, what have I learned in my more than forty years as an FBI agent and consultant engaged in objective fact finding? From a professional perspective, I learned that adults tend to believe what they want or need to believe – the greater the need, the greater the tendency. Therefore, possible bias must always be considered. I learned that variations in definitions could lead to alternative facts and confusion. And information is not accurate or true simply because friends, family, peers, supervisors, or clients say it is or we want it to be. Whether information emanates from a personal, political, or professional perspective can be important in evaluating its reliability and accuracy. I learned to strive for the professional or objective perspective in my work. Getting too emotionally involved can increase errors and interfere with objective analysis.

From a personal perspective, I learned the importance of striving for excellence. You never know how decisions and efforts in one area might unexpectedly affect other areas. The events of life are interrelated, and there are many forks in the road on the journey of life that lead us to where we wind up. The good grades I got in high school, college, Navy training, and FBI New Agent training opened doors and granted me opportunities I never anticipated. I learned that the kind of person you become is influenced by your genetic predispositions shaped by life experiences and the choices you make. I realized that my professional experiences could be meaningfully applied to important everyday decision-making. I learned that for me, it was more important to do the right thing as I saw it than to be rich or famous. I am still trying to learn, however, to stop screaming at the TV when I see so many commentators and pundits not doing what I have recommended in this book. My wife wishes I had learned.

Confirming some of what I learned on my journey, a 2016 study conducted by scholars at Stanford University Graduate School of Education found that students from middle school through college were easily duped by information online. In a 2017 follow-up report, the Stanford History Education Group found that unreliable website indicators often took in even skilled users, such as PhD historians with full-time faculty positions and Stanford University undergraduates. Somewhat echoing my law enforcement perspective, the report cautioned that when it comes to judging the credibility of information on the Internet, **skepticism** may be more useful than knowledge or old-fashioned research skills. Sam Wineburg, a co-author of the report said, "Very intelligent people were bamboozled by the ruses that are part of the toolkit of digital deception today." In a ray of hope for the future, lawmakers in several states have introduced or passed bills calling on public school systems to do more to teach media literacy skills that they say are critical to democracy. In co-sponsoring such a bill in Washington, Hans Zeiger, a Republican state senator, is quoted by the AP as saying, "There is such a thing as an objective source versus other kinds of sources, and that's an appropriate thing for schools to be teaching."

I was also recently gratified to read portions of speeches by two officials of the U. S. Department of Justice – where I worked for thirty years. I think these two brief comments summarize much of what I have communicated here.

FBI Director Christopher Wray spoke at the Ronald Reagan International Trade Center in Washington, DC, on October 19, 2017, as part of an annual award ceremony for inspectors general employees. He was quoted as saying, "At some point for everybody in this room and everybody in my organization, our integrity will be tested. It could be at a time where we're being asked to make a decision that is inconsistent with what we know is right and what we know is true, where we'll be asked to do something without fully thinking it through. I would argue that actually those are the times where we need to stay most true to our core integrity and our professionalism. To think critically and thoughtfully and to do what's right, not just for ourselves individually so we can look ourselves in the mirror as leaders, but for our agencies and the government and the public that we all serve."

Speaking at the Justice Department's Criminal Division Awards Ceremony in Washington, D.C. on December 12, 2017, Deputy Attorney General Rod Rosenstein was quoted as saying, "Promoting public confidence in our work is sometimes challenging, particularly in the modern era of nonstop so-called breaking news. Talking heads and commentators are not constrained by the need to find credible eyewitnesses and determine the facts beyond any reasonable doubt before reaching a verdict. Sometimes critics are not constrained by the facts at all."

In the end, my compelling desire to marry Kathy worked out well for me. We celebrated our 50th wedding anniversary in 2017. My journey with my wife, the love of my life, has been inspiring and fulfilling. Our two children grew up to be happy and self-sufficient adults. My journey through life has been bookended by two significant personally traumatic events – my father dying from cancer in 1962 when I was a teenager and my wife being diagnosed with stage IV cancer in 2016. In professional retirement, I continue the personal journey in my new position as my wife's primary care partner in her battle against cancer. It has been the most frustrating, difficult, and rewarding position I have ever had.

I realize that certain decisions I made along the way defined my life. Near the end of the movie *Scent of a Woman*, the character Lt. Col. Frank Slade (Al Pacino) articulates "Now I have come to the crossroads in my life. I always knew what the right path was. Without exception, I knew, but I never took it. You know why? It was too damn hard."

My family, religion, and life experiences taught me how to recognize that path. In my personal and professional journey, I am proud and satisfied with my efforts to take the right, difficult, and sometimes unpopular path. Of the three words in the FBI motto (fidelity, bravery, and integrity), the one that was the most important guidepost on my professional journey was *integrity*. Astronaut John

Young is quoted as having said in a 2000 interview, "You don't want to be politically correct, you want to be right." I know some might consider certain opinions and recommendations expressed here to be wrong or debatable, but they were sincerely arrived at through a thoughtful process developed over a long career of fact-finding. To paraphrase General Douglas MacArthur in his 1951 speech before Congress: I now close my professional career and just fade away, an old FBI agent who tried to do his duty as God and his family gave him the light to see that duty.

Appendix I

Clichés that Seem To Be True, but Aren't

1. "A missing child is any child who is not where he or she is supposed to be."
    (*See* Chapters Three & Seven)
2. "According to the FBI, one in four females will be sexually molested as a child."
    (*See* Chapter Three)
3. "The online sexual predator is today's version of the stranger in the playground."
    (*See* Chapter Seven)
4. "If you are being abducted, it is always best to resist and fight."
    (*See* Chapter Seven)
5. "Adults don't ask children for directions."
    (*See* Chapter Seven)
6. "Today, children are at greater risk of being abducted by sexual predators than ever before."
    (*See* Chapters Six & Seven)
7. "Everyone in the United States is an immigrant other than Native Americans."
    (*See* Chapter Ten)
8. "This is the first generation of children that will not be better off than their parent."
    (See Chapter Ten)
9. "Children are not supposed to die before their parents"
    (*See* Chapter Ten)
10. "The police cannot stop someone based on their race and appearance."

    (*See* Chapter Ten)

APPENDIX **II**

References and Recommended Reading

Andersen, K. (2017) *Fantasyland: how America went haywire: a 500-year history.* New York, NY: Random House.

Cheit, R.E. (2014). *The witch-hunt narrative.* New York, NY: Oxford University Press.

Franklin, H.G. (2005). *On bullshit.* Princeton, NJ: Princeton University Press.

Levitt, S.D. and Dubner, S. J. (2005). *Freakonomics.* New York, NY: HarperCollins.

Mintz, S. (2004). *Huck's raft: a history of American childhood.* Cambridge, MA: Harvard University Press.

Nathan, D. & Snedeker, M. (1995). *Satan's silence: ritual abuse and the making of a modern American witch hunt.* New York, NY: Basic Books.

Newberg, A. and Waldman, M.R. (2006). *Why we believe what we believe.* New York, NY: Free Press.

Restak, R.M. (1982). The self seekers: Understanding manipulators, the predominant personalities of our age. Garden City, NY: Doubleday & Company.

Sagan, C. (1996). *The demon-haunted world: science as a candle in the dark.* New York, NY: Random House.

Sedlak, A.J., Finkelhor, D., Hammer, H., and Schultz, D.J. (2002). "National Estimates of Missing Children: An Overview." *Juvenile Justice Bulletin*–NCJ196465, 1-12.

Tavris, C. and Aronson, E. (2007). *Mistakes were made (but not by me).* Orlando, FL: Harcourt Publishing.

Wheen, F. (2004). *How mumbo jumbo conquered the world.* New

York, NY: Perseus Books.

Wolak, J., Finkelhor, D., and Sedlak, A. (2016). : "Child Victims of Stereotypical Kidnappings Known to Law Enforcement in 2011." *Juvenile Justice Bulletin*, 1-20, Washington, DC: US Department of Justice, Office of Programs, Office of Juvenile Justice and Delinquency Prevention.

Wolak, J., Finkelhor, D., and Mitchell, K. (2004). Internet-initiated sex crimes against minors: Implications for prevention based on findings from a national study. *Journal of Adolescent Health*, 35, pp. 424.e11-424.e20.

Appendix III
References and Lanning Publications

The following are some of publications I have authored during my career that go into more detail on a number of the ideas and concepts concerning sexual victimization of children set forth in this book:

Lanning, K.V. & Burgess, A.W. (1984). Child pornography and sex rings. *FBI Law Enforcement Bulletin*, 53, 10-16.

Lanning, K.V. (1986). *Child molesters: A behavioral analysis*. Alexandria, VA: National Center for Missing & Exploited Children.

Lanning, K.V. (1987). *Child molesters: A behavioral analysis* (2nd Ed.). Alexandria, VA: National Center for Missing & Exploited Children.

Lanning, K.V. (1989). *Child sex rings: A behavioral analysis*. Alexandria, VA: National Center for Missing & Exploited Children.

Lanning, K.V. (1989). Satanic, occult, ritualistic crime: a law enforcement perspective. *The Police Chief*, LVI (10), 62-84

Lanning, K.V. (1991). Ritual abuse: a law enforcement view or perspective. *Child Abuse and Neglect: The International Journal*, 15, 171-173.

Lanning, K.V. (1992). *Investigator's guide to allegations of "ritual" child abuse*. Quantico, VA: U.S. Department of Justice.

Lanning, K.V. (1992). Satanic, occult, ritualistic crime: a law enforcement perspective. *Homicide Investigators Journal*, Spring.

Lanning, K.V. (1992). *Child sex rings: A behavioral analysis* (2nd Ed.). Alexandria, VA: National Center for Missing & Exploited Children.

Lanning, K.V. (1992). *Child molesters: A behavioral analysis* (3rd Ed.). Alexandria, VA: National Center for Missing & Exploited Children.

Lanning, K. V. (1994). Sexual homicide of children. *The APSAC Advisor*, Volume 7(4), 40-44.

Lanning, K. V. (1995). Investigative analysis and summary of teaching points. In K. V. Lanning & A. W. Burgess (Eds.), *Child molesters who abduct: Summary of the case in point series.* 17-36, Alexandria, VA: National Center for Missing & Exploited Children.

Lanning, K.V. (1996). Criminal investigation of sexual victimization of children. Briere, J., Berliner, L., Bulkley, J.A., Jenny, C., & Reid, T. (eds.). *The APSAC handbook on child maltreatment.* 247-264, Thousand Oaks, CA: SAGE.

Lanning, K.V. (1996). The "witch hunt," the "backlash," and professionalism. *The APSAC Advisor*, Volume 9(4), Winter, 8-11.

Lanning, K.V. (2001). *Child molesters: A behavioral analysis* (4th Ed.). Alexandria, VA: National Center for Missing & Exploited Children.

Lanning, K.V. (2005). Compliant child victim: Confronting an uncomfortable reality. E. Quayle and M. Taylor (Eds.), *Viewing child pornography on the Internet.* 49-60, Dorset, United Kingdom: Russell House Publishing.

Lanning, K.V. (2010). *Child molesters: A behavioral analysis* (5th Ed.). Alexandria, VA: National Center for Missing & Exploited Children. (Available from NCMEC as free download) (www.missingkids.org/ourwork/publications/exploitation/nc70)

Lanning, K.V. (2012). Twenty-five years of APSAC: a personal, historical law enforcement perspective. *The APSAC Advisor*, Vol 24, No 1 & 2.

Lanning, K.V. & Dietz, P.E. (2014). Acquaintance child molesters and youth-serving organizations. *Journal of Interpersonal Violence*, 29, 2815-2838.

Lanning, K.V. (2016). Sexual victimization of children: rape or molestation. Hazelwood, R.E. & Burgess, A.W. (eds.). *Practical Aspects of Rape Investigation.* 305-317, Boca Raton, FL: CRC Press (5th Ed).

Lanning, K.V. (2017). A commentary from a law enforcement perspective on the witch-hunt narrative of Ross Cheit. *Journal of Interpersonal Violence, 32*, No 6, 967-978.

Lanning, K.V. & Beasley, J.O. (2017). Child molesters who abduct: a behavioral analysis. Van Hasselt, V.B. & Bourke, M.L. (eds.). *Handbook of Behavioral Criminology.* 699-727, New York, NY: Springer Nature.

Lanning, K.V. (2018). The evolution of *grooming*: concept and term. *Journal of Interpersonal Violence*, 33, No 1, 5-16.

Prentky, R. A., Knight, R.A., Burgess, A. W., Ressler, R., Campbell, J., & Lanning, K. V. (1991). Child molesters who abduct. *Violence and Victims*, 6 (3), 213-224.

ABOUT THE AUTHOR

Mr. Lanning is currently a consultant in the area of crimes against children. Before retiring in 2000, he was a Special Agent with the FBI for more than 30 years. He was assigned to the FBI Behavioral Science Unit and the National Center for the Analysis of Violent Crime at the FBI Academy in Quantico, Virginia for 20 of those years (longer than any other agent doing behavioral analysis).

He is a founding member of the Board of Directors of the American Professional Society on the Abuse of Children (APSAC) and is a former member of the APSAC Advisory Board. He is a former member of the Advisory Board of the Association for the Treatment of Sexual Abusers (ATSA). Mr. Lanning is the 1990 recipient of the Jefferson Award for Research from the University of Virginia, the 1996 recipient of the Outstanding Professional Award from APSAC, the 1997 recipient of the FBI Director's Annual Award for Special Achievement for his career accomplishments in connection with missing and exploited children, and the 2009 recipient of the Lifetime Achievement Award for Outstanding Service from the National Children's Advocacy Center.

He has testified on seven occasions before the U.S. Congress and many times as an expert witness in state and federal court. Mr. Lanning has authored numerous publications and consulted on thousands of cases involving the sexual victimization of children. He has lectured before and trained tens of thousands of law enforcement officers, prosecutors, social workers, mental health and medical personnel, judges, and other professionals.

Made in the USA
Columbia, SC
17 September 2020